# TABLE OF CONTENTS

# <u>ACKNOWLEDGEMENTS</u>

First and foremost, I want to thank God for His infinite mercy and grace. He has always held my hands and has been a lamp to my feet. God's unconditional love has allowed me to go on when I felt like giving up. His sweet resounding voice has given me peace and hope, not only for myself, but for my daughter, Grace, and generations to come. God has taken me from a mighty long way, and I bless His Holy Name for those experiences as each decision has helped shape my perspective on life. Every step I have taken has led me to write this book. I hope when reading Chosen, you will know beyond a shadow of a doubt that you have been called, sanctified, and chosen to do great works!

I thank my husband, Shadson, for always encouraging me towards the high mark of God. To my parents and my sister, Natacha, you all have always put a smile on my face, and I thank you for being there for me in all moments of life.

Beth Zwecher, you have been instrumental to my growth. Apostle Pacific Zagabe, you have been a beacon of the Gospel, and through your ministry, I discovered my own.

To everyone who has ever spoken 'life' over my life, thank you. To Pastor Amos and his wife Marie Ange Jean-Phillipe, you both have been positioned as a catalyst for my ministry. I want to thank the members of WCOG for having been there since my arrival in the US. Thank you to Christina Dubique for being a great friend and contributor to the final product of this book.

A special thank you to my mentees who are growing in the faith. I hope when you read this book, your light will shine brighter. And to you who have decided to read this book, there is no doubt that you have been called by God to do great works. I hope by reading this book, you will be encouraged, strengthened and compelled to carry out those great works! You have been chosen.

# <u>Dedication</u>

I dedicate this book to my daughter, Grace Joyce
Merzius, a beam of hope, and a pure stream of light.
Grace, you have motivated me to dream bigger, think
better, and live wiser.

# PREFACE

Chosen is not just a book but rather my life story. This book has been planted as a seed in my heart since my teenage years and has bloomed ever since.

My mission and calling have been centered on helping young people find their purpose and to live in their truth. The book touches on epochs of my life that have had an impact on my spiritual journey. I have allowed my life, through this book, to be as vulnerable and honest as possible in the hopes of being able to help you discover *your truth.* As a young woman and a follower of Christ, my calling and earthly mission were not always clear. I often struggled to identify my purpose and sometimes, even fought the idea of having been called and most importantly, *chosen.*

Whether you feel it, believe or live it, you have been chosen to do great works through God, and have chosen to leave your mark on this world. But the journey of a called and chosen person is not always easy. Through my journey of discovery, I sometimes struggled, doubted, feared and failed a couple of times. All of these moments, however, have built my character, my understanding of God and has strengthened my pursuit of Him.

In this journey, you will have to let some people go. Sometimes, you will feel alone, misunderstood, and even left out of the crowd. You will be faced with hard and life-altering choices. The reality is, there is a reason you chose this book. Something propelled you to read *Chosen* because deep inside, you know you were created for greater things.

You were *chosen* for such a time as this, and it is time you stand up and walk in this truth. You have gifts, talents, dreams, goals, and purpose sitting right inside of you. I hope this book will give you a fresh perspective and will help in the activation and fulfillment of these things.

Use this book as a guide. Within these chapters, you will find pertinent testimonies, guidance for your spiritual life and hopefully, relatable experiences to help guide you in the light of Christ.




You did not choose me, but I chose you and appointed you that you should go and bear fruit and that your fruit should abide, so that whatever you ask the Father in my name, he may give it to you.



*John 15:16*

# <u>OPENING PRAYER</u>

Dear God, I thank you for your word which is a lamp to our feet and a light on our path. You are the author of wisdom, clarity, and from your mouth comes knowledge. Help me to retain your word as I put them into application in my life. Open my spiritual eyes that I may see and experience your fullness. Through this book, I will receive revelation, insight, and Kingdom understanding. In Jesus' Name I pray, Amen.

*Lord, I come to you now, with a humble heart and a contrite spirit. I thank you for my humble beginnings because I know your purpose for my life is not tied to my small beginnings. I know according to your word, your plans for me are more than I will ever be able to understand. I know you, Lord, have given me divine access into your heart through your word. Your plans for my life are great, and I know this well. Allow me the patience to wait and work towards your perfect Will for my life. In your name I pray. Amen.*

"Your beginnings will seem humble, so prosperous will your future be."

*Job 8:7*

# HUMBLE BEGINNINGS

Jesus was born in a manger, one of the most humble circumstances imaginable. He came from Heaven to earth, leaving all of His Glory and power to share our lives and even the temptations of this world. His parents were from Nazareth, and according to John 1:46, nothing good ever came from Nazareth. He could have come in the form of His Glory with Angels marching and Seraphim bowing. He chose, however, to come in the likeness of man so that we can see ourselves in Him. Jesus came as a meek and vulnerable baby, who suffered alongside us for the sake of His Gospel. The Bible states:

> Although He existed in the form of God, did not regard equality with God a thing to be grasped, but emptied Himself, taking the form of a bond-servant, and being made in the likeness of men. Being found in appearance as a man, He humbled Himself by becoming obedient to the point of death, even death on a cross. For this reason also, God highly exalted Him, and bestowed on Him the name which is above every name (Philippians 2:6–9).

Jesus left His eternal fellowship with God in Heaven to become a Savior for you and me. His humble birth is one that many can relate to, yet others try to overlook. You might not

11

have been birthed in the greatest circumstances or have a wealthy upbringing. Perhaps you have made some decisions that have impacted your character and how others view you. God, however, takes the humble and crushed things of this world to make them great. God is still in the business of restoring, changing and making the least of us great. It is not too late for you to start over. Do not let your past define where you are headed.

---

> God takes the humble things of this
> world and makes them great.

---

The Bible takes us through very detailed accounts of its vivid and relatable characters. David, having one of the most humble beginnings, became King of a great Nation and united the people of Israel. He not only led them to victory in battle but also paved the way for his son, Solomon, who later built the Holy Temple. David was a man after God's own heart. He was the youngest of his brothers, and so, in the natural mind of man, he was not fit nor qualified to be king, but God had other plans.

Isn't it amazing when people think you're done with, they write you off, and God says, "No, I am not through with them yet," and shows His glory? Saul was the first king of the Israelites, but after leading them for about twenty-five years, he sinned so much that God sent His prophet Samuel to anoint a future king who would be his successor.

From a human standpoint, there are times when God's choices defy our logic. Unlike his siblings, David was not always in the public eye and was often forgotten and misunderstood. When Prophet Samuel was sent by God to find the next king of Israel, seven of Jesse's sons presented but God chose none of them; that is, until David, the forgotten one, showed up. Like David, society may have overlooked your gifts, talents, calling, and ministry. Maybe you know you have been called to a specific dimension, and your friends, family members, pastors, and people from your surroundings have not yet identified who you are. But God, your creator and the finisher of your faith knows and sees you. The kingdom of God works according to time. Everything is done according to its specific timing and due season.

A blessing given too soon is not a blessing at all and a gift exposed too early may wreak havoc. God gives us hopes and dreams for certain things to happen in our lives, but He doesn't always allow us to know the exact timing of His plan. We can, sometimes, feel as if we have been forgotten and left out of the plan. This can be frustrating to those who are eager to live out according to God's will. Waiting is not always easy, and it can feel impossible, but in waiting, God builds our patience and deepens our intimacy with Him.

Through the waiting seasons in our lives, we learn about the compassion and faithfulness of God. We learn to be patient as we ardently wait to hear His voice.

After being anointed by the prophet Samuel, David went on his merry way back to tending his sheep. It is important to understand that nothing worth having ever comes easy or without opposition and preparation. Although David was called and anointed, his time had not yet arrived. He was anointed but not yet appointed. His humble beginnings were fermenting his call to be King.

---

In Waiting, God builds our patience
and deepens our intimacy with Him

---

Too often, we allow the wait in-between to affect our view of what is to come. Many times, we allow our upbringing to affect the way we view ourselves and our potential. If David had focused on how he was a shepherd boy and not on his calling to be king, he would have never leaped forward to lead the nation. You have a unique DNA that determines your genetic and spiritual makeup. Because of this, your experiences, struggles, victories differ greatly from those around you. Don't be surprised if no one "gets" you. Don't be surprised if you're overlooked and underestimated.

Your starting line may not have been the best, and sure, you may have had some hiccups along the way, those things, however, do not have to define who you are in Christ. The Bible says, "Therefore, if anyone is in Christ, the new creation has come: The old has gone, the new is here" (2 Corinthians 5:17). You are a new person, and God is not keeping tabs on all of the wrongs you have done.

---

## David was anointed but not yet appointed.

---

Prophet Jeremiah was another instrument God appointed to bring His people out of captivity. Jeremiah was from the small village of Anathoth, a territory of Benjamin (Jeremiah 1:1). As a young boy, God called Jeremiah by name and stamped him for ministry. God gave Jeremiah the overview of his prophetic ministry: "Behold, I have put My words in your mouth. See, I have this day set you over the nations and over the kingdoms, to root out and to pull down, to destroy and to throw down, to build and to plant" (Jeremiah 1: 9-10). Although Jeremiah was young and did not come from an elite family, God used him to warn the people of their sins and to warn them to repent from their sinful ways. God's words became like fire in his heart. Jeremiah was on fire for God and was unable to hold this fire for himself.

The word of God says in Jeremiah 29:11, "For I know the plans I have for you," declares the Lord, "plans to prosper you and not to harm you, plans to give you hope and a future." No matter the country, neighborhood, social class, school, or family you come from, God's plan for you is as great as it was for David and prophet Jeremiah. God has a plan to prosper your life for His Glory.

Your upbringing may not have been the best, but God, who is omniscient, sees the end from the beginning and knows the beginning from the end. He manufactured every one of us for greatness, and He alone holds the very parts to our destiny. You were not an afterthought. Your humble beginnings will be used to propel you to your God-given destiny.

---

## God has a plan to prosper your life for His Glory.

---

I grew up in a little pink house just outside of Port-au-Prince. Les Cayes has bustling main streets, a sprightful culture, and lively people. Its rolling mountains are covered with lush trees, and rivers run for miles ending at the blue basin. Haiti's intoxicating cuisine, intricate architecture, and colorful art draw in people from all over the world.

Living in Haiti, my mornings were filled with roosters crowing and the sounds of peaceful streams. My days entailed snatching mangos from trees and my afternoons, racing friends down the lagoon. At night, I would sit by the trees in my backyard to catch coconuts while my mother read Biblical stories. Life was like a melody, and it was a sweet sound.

As time went on, the mangos stopped falling, the coconuts were no longer a muse, and the lagoon dried up. The little things that made me happy no longer satisfied. Soon afterward, my mother and I moved to the main city in the hopes of furthering my education. Life, which once seemed so tranquil, became unsettling. My grandfather, who was a pillar in our family, went to Heaven. The same year, my father moved to the United States leaving behind the memories shared. Adjusting to this new life was nothing short of challenging.

My mother, now living as a single mother, worked twice as hard to provide for my needs. Every day, she sew clothes to sell in the marketplace. After standing for long hours in the scorching sun, she would come home with sunburns on her forehead and arms. The gleam in her eyes faded. Wrinkles started to form, and suddenly, her favorite skirt no longer fit. She was thinning right before my eyes.

With the money earned from her days in the market, my mother was able to pay for school. Life was not the easiest, but we had hope. I remember the rain dripping through our tin roof, soaking our sleeping mat. The city was not the ideal place to live. Violence and crime was the norm, and the spirit of destruction raided the nation.

We grew fearful for our lives, moving from house to house and eventually settling at an aunt's house. Although we were not well off financially, my mother was a warrior in the spirit, and the word of God was her sword. My days consisted of morning, midday, and nightly prayers. Early in the morning, before the city awoke, my mother would gather along with other sentinels to pray. Their prayers were enough to shake the city.

Sunday mornings, I came alive. I loved church and was fascinated by the word of God. While others would dread the long morning walks to church, I was eager about being in the presence of God. The five-mile walk was a breeze. One Sunday, after being asked to sing in the routine musical selection at church, the pastor decided there was no more time allotted for me to sing; I cried. After such embarrassment, he allowed me the opportunity to sing, and I stretched out every second on the pulpit. I was seven years old, and all I wanted to do was praise God. As silly as that illustration is, there was nowhere better to be than at church.

As I grew older, however, I began to feel a void. This time, it was different from the void I felt leaving Les Cayes. This void was not familiar. There was a yearning and a strong desire to dig in deeper. It wasn't long after I realized this was the tugging of the Holy Spirit. He wanted to introduce Himself in a way like never before. He not only wanted me to know *about* Him, but God also wanted me to *know* Him for myself.

After my early years of living in Haiti, I moved to the United States joining my father, leaving behind the one true comfort I had ever known; my mother. The years of transition were some of the most difficult years of my life. Life was faster, people were busier, and to most, God seemed to be an afterthought. People did not seem to pray as much, and the church I attended, needless to say, seemed powerless. No one at home seemed to live a life of prayer.

The desire and eagerness to know God started to dim. I was culture shocked and could not believe how different the US was from my homeland. School was dreadful. In middle school, I was bullied for my pigtails and for not being up to date with the times. My skirts were longer than most, and I could not afford the new sidekick phones and every day was a nightmare, causing me to become distant and alone. I suffered in silence while being yelled at, pushed and other times kicked by the other girls in my grade. I developed a coping mechanism for meditation and prayer. For years, I battled with depression, and I questioned my existence and sometimes, even God.

I felt hopeless and helpless. I had nowhere to go and nowhere to turn but God. The days turned to months and months to years. Finally, I was on my way to high school where everything was supposed to be better. It was not. In fact, things worsened.

My spiritual life plummeted while my social life bloomed. Although I kept very few friends, they were not

17

good role models. Because of the strict structure at home, I was not allowed the liberty of my peers. I had a strict curfew and seldom was allowed to go out with friends. I began lying to my parents about my whereabouts and hung out with the wrong people. Although not easily influenced, I made the wrong decisions often thinking my friends and the choices I made would fill the emptiness I felt.

Wanting to experience some sort of a thrill, I embarked in a relationship at the age of fifteen. Without consulting God, I decided he was going to be the one I'd spend my happy ever after with. Everything about him seemed right. He said the right things, and for sure, I had made up in my naïve mind that he was going to be my Boaz. I tried to convince myself that he would bring happiness, but he did not. Instead, I was mentally and verbally abused regularly. I was often pushed to make decisions that were outside of myself, and for months, I compromised my faith and my morals. I allowed myself to be consumed by the flesh and regularly stepped out of the will of God. The Bible says in 1 John 3:6, "Those who live in Christ don't go on sinning. Those who go on sinning haven't seen or known Christ." I did not *know* Christ.

I had heard about this great and mighty Savior but had not yet met Him for myself. After months of compromising my beliefs, I suddenly realized that God most certainly had better plans for my life. There was always a still small voice reminding me of my worth and my value in Christ. I knew there had to be more to life than the lies and the compromise.

The enemy made me feel insignificant and not loved. I felt as though God would never use me because of my brokenness. I couldn't have been more wrong. As his threats grew stronger, God's grace grew even more. I found myself in the arms of God, pouring my heart about wanting to be liberated and freed. The depression lessened, and I began to think about my potential in Christ.

One day, I finally grew the strength to stand up and fight. I fought against the negative thoughts of "you're worthless," "you're not loved," "God can't use you," and I won. Sometimes, the guilt we feel from the fall is worse than the actual fall itself. I had spent months beating myself over sins I had committed against God.

The devil has a way of reminding us of our forgiven past. He tries to display our shortcomings, mistakes, and sins every chance he gets. The beauty of our relationship with Christ is, once we have confessed our sins and have received the forgiveness of the Lord, God does not keep a trail on our past sins. We have a father in Heaven who is gracious, merciful, and compassionate towards us. The Bible tells us in Psalm 103:12, "As far as the east is from the west, so far has he removed our transgressions from us."

After being convicted of my wrong ways of living, I had to decide to live better. Many people think the devil does not know what we are called to do but that is false. Satan has an idea about what you have been called to do in the kingdom and will stop at nothing until he tries to stop you. Your life is too precious to be wasted in fear and compromise. I made a decision that forever changed my life; for the better.

One question I usually bring to my Sunday school class is, "Is the sin you're living in really worth your eternal blessing?" There is a level that God is calling us to that will make living righteously a lifestyle. The Bible says in 1 Corinthians 10:13, "No temptation has overtaken you except what is common to mankind. And God is faithful; he will not let you be tempted beyond what you can bear. But when you are tempted, he will also provide a way out so that you can endure it." This should give us hope in knowing that no matter the sin, God has given us the antidote which is the blood of the Lamb! Once we enter into a true communion with Christ, the urges of the flesh should lessen. Some have struggled with the same sin for decades because there has not really been repentance. By confessing and repenting, the Grace of God then takes over, aligning us once more with our call to destiny. Beautiful things happen when we allow the Holy Spirit to convict us of our wrongs. As sons and daughters of Christ, His Spirit is in us, and He guides us in the way we should go. Because God's purpose for us is to prosper, we can rest knowing that if we put our lives in the hands of this great Creator, He will never lead us astray.

The Holy Spirit is a comforter and brings peace to our circumstances, minds, and He enriches our beings. His Spirit does not force nor does it bring confusion. I was searching for instant gratification and was obsessed with the feeling of being *loved* that I missed out on the true love of God. It was not until I ran into the arms of a loving God that I realized the world had nothing to offer me; not happiness, not gratification and certainly not *love.*

Every decision we make shapes our outlook on the world. Before meeting Jesus Christ, I was a broken little girl seeking love from all of the wrong things in this world. It was not until I discovered *my truth* and started to live out my purpose that I realized my identity and all that comes with what was hidden in God. I had to get to know my maker. God has a marvelous way of choosing the "foolish things of the world to shame the wise; God chose the weak things of the world to shame the strong" (1 Corinthians 1:27).

No matter how small your beginnings were or how broken you may have been in the past, God is a restorer of things. He can give you full restoration and put the pieces back together if you will allow Him to. Just like David and Prophet Jeremiah, God has a specific calling attached to your name. No other person can fulfill that role but you. If looking at the characters in the Bible, every one of them had issues, sins, and were nowhere near perfect.

They realized that in their strengths, they were not capable, but through God, they were unshakable. Perhaps in your past, you struggled with an addiction that tries to come back into your life from time to time.

Maybe you have had a rough time recovering from continuous sinful habit. It is important to understand the importance of true repentance. If you have truly repented and believe in your heart that through Jesus, you have been forgiven, sin has lost its power and has no legal right in your life! A life of sin is not only hurtful to your spiritual life but is demonic and needs to be treated as so. Stop making excuses and cast out the spirit and be freed in Jesus' Name! It is time you live in your truth in order to fulfill your God-given destiny.

*Beautiful things happen when we are convicted by the Holy Spirit.*

*God, I thank you for having chosen me. You knew me when I was in my mother's womb, and you created me with a great purpose and plan. I know that the work you have begun in me, you will complete. I believe in your plan for my life, and I surrender the journey to you. In Jesus' Name I pray. Amen.*

"For I know the plans I have for you," declares the Lord, "plans to prosper you and not to harm you, plans to give you hope and a future."

*Jeremiah 29: 11*

# THE JOURNEY

There is something about a journey that is exciting and invigorating. It is a promise of new possibilities yet many challenges. Our spiritual journey is one that is personal, intimate, and always growing. Through our walk, God unfolds the secrets of His kingdom and reveals His desires to us. Psalm 34:4 tells us to take delight in the Lord, and He will give us the desires of our hearts. I believe this is a two-dimensional promise: God will not only let us have what our hearts desire but He Himself will put His desires in our hearts.

A desire is not whimsical; it is deeper than that. In our spiritual journey, we should ardently seek to have intimacy with God that we may know what His purpose and plans are for our lives. Before you were even born, The Great, Mighty, and All-Powerful Creator saw that *you* would be a great addition to this world. He knitted you and designed every part of your life.

Imagine a car manufacturer. When creating a car, manufacturers know exactly which parts are needed in order to make the car a great one. They assemble the parts, both the one's eyes can see and the ones hidden so the car may have excellent performance. Although not on the same scale, God has given you the correct 'parts' needed to fulfill your purpose here on earth.

---

There is only one you in the world
and you were beautifully, wonderfully
knitted together!

---

One of the most beautiful things God requires of us is a relationship. For years, I thought singing church hymns, going to every prayer meeting meant that I had a close relationship with God. Although I was doing all of these things, I was not living righteously. I took part in all the wrong things and hung with the wrong crowd. I knew religion but had no idea what relationship was. Our relationship with God is the best thing in our lives and takes precedence over everything else. But how can we be intimate with God if we do not know Him? The start of our walk with Christ begins once we seek to know who He is. The time spent with God will allow us to be vulnerable and will let us become more attentive to His desires and interests.

God's ultimate purpose for us is to know Him and most importantly, to be saved through His Son, Jesus Christ, that we may reign in Glory with Him. Satan has deceived many by portraying the Gospel of Jesus through sin. Sin is real and is a horrible thing. At some point, we each have had to deal with a particular sin but the Grace of God always predominates. Jesus' ministry calls us to repentance and conversion. In John 3:3, Jesus Christ says that, unless we are born again, we cannot see the Kingdom of God.

This shows us that the conversion experience is a requirement if we want to go to Heaven. The truth is, who we are now is not who we should be. We are all works in progress and designs being mastered in the hands of a great Artist. We are sinners from the ground up and only a great Savior can change and mend our circumstances. We need to change, but we cannot rescue, redeem and save ourselves. The Holy Spirit is not only the principle agent to this change but is also our incubator. The trajectory of the Christian life is one that encompasses conversion, ongoing reflection, and repentance. In our journey, we will fall and sometimes in our fall, it may feel as though our sins are stronger than the love and grace of God. But Jesus Christ has defeated sin and the Cross testifies of this. That is why, when we step out of the will of God, we are not merely breaking a 'law' but are really betraying and rejecting our relationship with Christ.

One of my great friends back in undergrad moved to California sophomore year. Over the years, we kept in touch, but the distance grew longer, and the phone calls grew shorter until eventually, we lost contact. Six years later, I saw her at the beach. As excited as I was to see her, it was strange. We had missed so many details in each other's lives that we did not know where to start. I married and had a daughter, and she had moved back to Massachusetts and was pursuing a career completely different from her studies. The conversation was sweet and short. Although we exchanged numbers, I knew we would never be the same again.

If our earthly relationships are like this, we can expect the same for our relationship with Christ. For many of us, when we first become Christians, we are motivated and zealous towards the Gospel of our Lord Jesus Christ. As time goes by, however, we get too comfortable, and we lose sight of the true prize which is our salvation. Most become lazy and stop praying and reading the Word. They live their everyday lives on an empty spiritual tank only to be filled on Sunday mornings.

God does not need nor does He want a "once a week Sunday morning" relationship with you! He wants you every day of the week. As we understand this, praying, fasting and reading the word becomes first nature. Spending quality time in the presence of God will allow us to understand who He is. By understanding who He is, our love for Him will grow and will motivate us to be obedient to His voice.

I was twelve years old when I accepted the Lord Jesus Christ as my personal Lord and Savior. In the basement of a church, I kneeled down as the pastor's wife prayed with me. Why I made that decision then, I'm not sure. However, I knew the decision would forever change my life. My journey with God is one that has been beautiful, rewarding, challenging, but always purposeful. In my Christian walk, I have made mistakes and have many times stepped out of God's will intentionally and most of the time, nay. That morning, in the basement of a small church, I received eternal life. This was a radical decision. This choice was not based on emotions but was a heartfelt, spirit-led cry to be saved.

For us to be effective in our journey, we have to be tactful and radical in our approach. There is an adversary who seeks to detour us from Heaven. He distracts us with complacency, vanity, and everything else this world has to offer. Many have become so busy in everyday life pursuits that God has become a figment of thought. For intimacy to take place, we must be persistent and consistent in meditating on the word of God, worship, prayer, and fasting.

---

Nothing worth having comes easy or without preparation.

---

The Bible gives us thorough detail on the lives of major patriarchs in the Bible. Abraham, the father of those who believe, in his journey, had to leave his country and follow God to an unknown land. I am sure Abraham was not screaming with joy when he found out he had to leave the place where he was comfortably and pleasantly living.

According to Hebrews 11, Abraham lived in Ur. The city at the time bustled with commerce, beautiful parks, and public buildings. He was living rather comfortably and secure in Ur. However, the city was filled with paganism. God directed Abraham to leave and to dwell in tents for the rest of his life. What would you have done in this situation?

Abraham had to trust God for his provision, guidance, and protection. He not only had faith, but he obeyed God. Hebrews 11:8 records, "By faith Abraham, when called to go to a place he would later receive as his possession, obeyed and went, even though he did not know where he was going." His obedience to the prophetic program of God helped him reach the Promised Land.

In our personal journeys with God, our fears will be confronted. Many times, God will ask that we make decisions in our walk with Him that seems drastic and uncomfortable. Those decisions will test our faith, character, and desires to follow Christ. He intends to refine us so that we may be prepared for our Land of Promise. Nothing worth having comes easy or without preparation.

In the Book of Ezekiel, the prophet details a vision of the valley of bones. In Ezekiel 37, we read that God Himself set Ezekiel down in the middle of the valley of dry bones. There was no sign of life. The reviving of the dry bones was symbolic of God's plan for Israel. The nation had fallen away from God in sin and rebellion, so God withdrew His protection and blessings. Ezekiel wrote:

> "The hand of the Lord was on me, and he brought me out by the Spirit of the Lord and set me in the middle of a valley; it was full of bones. He led me back and forth among them, and I saw a great many bones on the floor of the valley, bones that were very dry. He asked me, "Son of man, can these bones live?" I said, "Sovereign Lord, you alone know
> (Ezek. 37:1-3).

28

I am sure Ezekiel did not know how to make the bones live, but he knew who did. God made them live. God, being full of mercy, promised that He would restore Israel by giving them life and filling them with His Spirit, making them His people.

Ezekiel's vision of the valley of dry bones is addressed to such a lifeless and hopeless frame of mind. How many dry bones do you have in your life? We all, at one point, have found ourselves in a valley. The valleys of fear, spiritual struggles, low self-esteem, financial insecurities, peer pressure, divorce, and instability are areas of inconsistency that test who we are in Christ.

---

Our obedience to the prophetic program of God will help us reach the Promised Land.

---

Ephesians 3:20 tells us, "Now to him who is able to do immeasurably more than all we ask or imagine, according to his power that is at work within us." The key word is *according* to His work in us. To the extent that He's allowed to work in us, will be the extent that He does great things through us. In the valley, many die spiritually and mentally because they refuse to die to themselves. In this journey, we are to die to ourselves, allowing God to take complete control of our hopes, dreams, desires, and future.

We each have to go through seasons of refining and shaping. In such seasons, it is easy to forget that the loving hands of God are wrapped around us. Pressures of this life take away our focus on the cross and magnify the dry bones. We have to believe in God's process as much as we trust and hope for His rewards. During such times, it helps if we remind ourselves that God loves us and His plans for us surpasses our imaginations. We can walk in our valleys confidently, not because we're perfect, but because He is!

The enemy can utilize everything, even the good things given by God, to distract people from God's purpose. The things we allow in our lives can very much distract us from having intimacy with God. Some of them are not necessarily bad in nature, but when our jobs, that television show, school, friends, and the marriage divert our focus from God, they become detrimental to our spiritual progress. Below are four of the biggest distractions Christians may face in their daily lives. If not handled properly, they can leave a lasting negative impact on our purpose and destiny.

1. Money
2. Media
3. Relationships
4. Religion

How did money make the list? Don't we all need money to live comfortably? Having money is not a sin, and it is not a hindrance; however, the *love* of money is. God gives us many material things because we need them to exist. These things, however, are for the fulfillment of God's purpose that Christ be wrought into man. Too many people work hard to buy things they don't need, with money they don't have, to impress people who will never care.

Greed for money causes people to do all sorts of things they wouldn't normally do. It motivates people to lie, steal, cheat, gamble, and even murder. Jesus said, "No one can serve two masters, for either he will hate the one and love the other, or he will be devoted to the one and despise the other. You cannot serve God and money" (Matthew 6:24).

Many people idolize the material things of this world which keeps them away from serving the one true King—Jesus Christ. We need to be aware of this and let go of the things of this world.

> Letting go is not always easy, but is
> certainly necessary.

We live today in an age of unprecedented distraction, and we have become conditioned to it all. It is not only harmful to our ability to listen and think carefully but also to our motivation to pray, fast, and meditate. The media has shifted the focus of many to tablets, televisions, and high tech phones. Distractions reveal what we love.

If we are not able to control the urge of opening up a social media page, then that says a lot about the core of who we are. Colossians 3:1-2 reminds us to set our hearts on things above. "Since, then, you have been raised with Christ, set your hearts on things above, where Christ is, seated at the right hand of God. Set your minds on things above, not on earthly things." As these distractions come, we have to be mindful that our time is unrecoverable.

In our busyness, we have to check our hearts. The Holy Spirit can help us see the nature of our hearts and assist us in regaining focus towards what really matters. Our relationships help us connect with the world, and they are normal to have. We shelter relationships with our parents, siblings, friends, husbands and wives, co-workers, and managers. When we allow any one of these relationships to become more important to us than our relationship with God, they become a distraction.

There are the right kind of relationships and also the wrong kind. Surrounding yourself with negative people will only attract negative circumstances. This is not only a distraction but spiritual suicide. God is able to give us a discerning spirit to identify who the distractions are in our lives. Once we are aware, we should take proper measures to let those people go and get rid of the dead weight. This can be painful and can sometimes seem impossible to do. However, ask yourself this question: is this relationship really worth me losing Heaven? Letting go is not always easy, but is certainly necessary.

Religion can also be a distraction. In Galatians 1:15-16, we have an illustration of a person who was seeking God yet was distracted. Paul was zealous for the Jewish religion, and he was ready to sacrifice his life for it—"I was advancing in Judaism beyond many of my own age among my people and was extremely zealous for the traditions of my fathers. But when God, who set me apart from my mother's womb and called me by his grace, was pleased to reveal his Son in me so that I might preach him among the Gentiles, my immediate response was not to consult any human being." Christ was revealed in Paul, and his life forever changed. Once he realized that his focus was in the wrong place, he shifted gears and set his eyes on the cross.

God has not called us to religion but has called for us to have a relationship with Him. God desires a relationship with you! He could care less if we are chanting scriptures and hymns. He wants our hearts to be right with Him first.

Distractions of this world will only do one thing—keep us from the Grace and Glory of God. Jesus Christ has already won the victory for you and me. On Calvary, He said: "It is finished!" On the cross, He took our shame, pain, loss, failures, sickness, and paved the way for us to be free from all of these distractions. You cannot go on this journey alone. If you allow Him, He will wrap Himself around you and will be your guide.

The decision to follow Christ is one that is essential to your walk with Him. Accepting Jesus Christ into your life is the best decision you will ever make. Romans 10:9 says, "If you shall confess with your mouth the Lord Jesus, and shall believe in your heart that God has raised him from the dead, you shall be saved." Jesus Christ died on the cross to pay the price for your sins. But He has given you free will to choose Him as your Savior and be forgiven of those sins.

Your journey with God begins with accepting that He loved you so much that He sent His Son to die on the cross for you. By accepting Him, you acknowledge this truth and are joined with Him for a lifelong intimate, enjoyable and fruitful journey.

*We have to believe in God's process as much as
we trust and hope for His rewards.*

*Lord, I thank you for your Holy Spirit which produces faith in us. Father, I pray that you will allow me tangible experiences that will not only build up my faith, but that will dry up any source of fear in my life. I know you have set me free from the spirit of fear and have called me in your Grace and Love. I pray, Lord, that you will consume my mind, thoughts, and spirit. Take complete control of my being and allow my mind to be freed from fear, failure, and condemnation. I reclaim my mind through the word of God. Lord, allow me the power to overcome and be victorious through your name, Jesus Christ. Amen.*

"For God has not given us a spirit of fear, but of power and of love and of a sound mind."

2 Timothy 1:7

# **FAITH OVER FEAR**

We all experience fear at some point in our lives. Someone once said, "Fear is false evidence appearing real." This pretty much sums up the devil's tactics in one sentence. By definition, fear is a response which seeks to avoid threatening danger. Some fears are natural while others are not. Very early on, a baby learns the difference between a quiet and a loud crowd. This type of fear which is built very early on is not necessarily bad. In fact, it can protect us from imminent danger.

However, in 2 Timothy 1:7, Apostle Paul alludes to another type of fear; one that is unnatural. The word *spirit* in Greek is *"pneuma,"* meaning wind or breath. This kind of fear is not normal and does not come from God. The spirit of fear is a portal to other demonic spirits, and if not identified early, it can keep one from reaching their God-given destiny. Although it comes in many forms, its intent is clear—to hinder your purpose.

Paul says God has given us the spirit of power. The word power in Greek is *dunamis*, and it is referred to over 160 times in the New Testament. This power is not any kind of power; it is an inherent power to do miraculous works through God. In Luke 4:36, we are painted a picture of a battle between the power of God and impure spirits: "All the people were amazed and said to each other, 'What words these are! With authority and power he gives orders to impure spirits and they come out!' This inherent power is in you to do marvelous things, including casting out of spirits and overcoming fear.

When I was in college, a good friend of mine was afraid of being out past the hour of 7 PM. It was one of the most bizarre situations. Because of this fear, she missed out on activities, projects, movie nights, ice cream socials, and even classes. At first, some of our friends thought this was due to religion, but it was not. When Khamaya was fifteen, she witnessed her mother die in a car crash; the hour of the accident, 7 PM. For years, she harbored the fear that this particular hour was some sort of a bad omen and the same thing would happen to her if she were out past this time. This fear had a rippling effect, and it crippled her spiritual, emotional, and social life.

Our mind is a battlefield, but God always wins. Once she faced the truth and realized that this fear was not normal, she sought help through prayer and was able to overcome this demonic spirit.

Fear is not an emotion. It is a demonic spirit and must be treated as such. The spirit of fear can be anything from not believing in God's timing for you to get married, have children, and go forth in ministry, to the fear of dying or fear of being sick. Many are confused on the difference between the fear of God and the spirit of fear. These two concepts are polar opposites. Having the fear of the Lord will actually take away the spirit of fear given that we abide in God's truth. This same power raised Jesus from the dead! That is dynamic power.

No demon in hell can stand against
the power of God!

Every time we try to rush God's plan for our lives, we are motivated by the spirit of fear. Forcing that relationship to work, living in the city God has told you not to live in or even staying in that career path God has told you to venture from, all of these decisions are motivated by fear. Many fear tomorrow because they forget that God is the author and finisher of our faith. He knows the end from the beginning and is continually working through us to perfect His plan and purpose.

Having a sound mind means being rational and having complete peace. Over half of the spiritual battle happens in our minds. The devil works to occupy our minds with lies, confusion, and more lies—after all, he is the father of lies. But your power and authority come from God, and no demon in hell can stand against the power of God.

One of the first steps to being free from the spirit of fear is acknowledging that the spirit actually exists. Once identified, its position must be nullified and voided. According to Matthew 18:18, we have the power to bind and loose things on this earth and in Heaven. Whatever we declare with our mouths and believe in our hearts will be done unto us! Whatever the place of fear is in your life, you have to command it to be broken in Jesus' Mighty Name. You have to speak directly to the spirit and demand it loose its grounds.

A couple of years ago, I was harassed by a recurring thought that I knew from the beginning was a demonic force. It made me uncomfortable and actually made me feel ashamed. I was afraid to speak to anyone about these thoughts; so, one day, I decided enough was enough. I went straight into the battlefield, with my sword *(Word of God)* and shield *(faith)* at hand. Demonic powers fight to keep their place. They are not easy to overthrow. With the blood of Jesus, however, they are powerless. I had to revoke every lie the enemy had sown into my mind. I confronted and spoke to the spirit out loud. I applied the blood of Jesus Christ and reminded the devil of its future *(see Revelations 20:10)*. It fled!

As sons and daughters of Christ, we have the power to overrule, bind, loose, and rebuke. That is a lot of power. Yet, many are unaware of this power that lies inside. A study done in the late 1900s argued that we only use 10% of our brain—that is absurd!

In the same way, many Christians are only using 10% of their power in Christ Jesus. Many people today strive to attain peace, wisdom and good judgment through behavioral sciences and other worldly practices. Unfortunately, this more times than not welcomes more demonic forces. On a spiritual level, a sound mind only comes through the Holy Spirit. Receiving the gifts of the Holy Spirit will allow us the discernment for what is right and wrong. They will also equip us against worry, doubt, and fear.

After graduating from Bentley University, I made up in my mind that I was going to open my own business and work for myself. The fear of not having the financial backup, time, and energy crept in. Suddenly, I became anxious and unsure of my future. I knew I wanted to open my business so I could devote my time to ministry. I struggled to develop the plan because I had already allowed the spirit of fear to come into my heart. Although I had my degree and had a vision in mind, I felt stuck.

I was working a 9 to 5 job and felt purposeless. My passion for serving through ministry became a distant thought. When purpose comes knocking on the doors of our hearts, we have to let it in. I remember spending weeks praying for God to open doors for my ministry, not realizing that He had opened the doors, I just had not walked through them. There I was with a degree from one of the best business schools in the nation, waiting for opportunities to come to me—I was blind, but the Holy Spirit opened my eyes.

I had to create the opportunity, despite the fears, the anxiety, and the naysayers. I had to decide to create the future

I dreamed. The desire to open my own business never went away. The need grew stronger and stronger.

One day, I decided I was going to make it happen. Unaware of how the journey would unfold, I ordered my first set of business cards and was on the journey to something greater than I could have imagined. Two weeks later, I opened my first business, Reconciled Business Services, LLC.

With any plan, there needs to be preparation and calculation. A lack of preparation can cause fear. Some may argue that success is when preparation meets opportunity. I can think of how each major decision I have made has been interwoven in the blueprint of my destiny. Preparation preceded each one of those major life decisions. A friend of mine once said, "Preparedness is an antidote to fear." I recall a sermon I preached at a youth revival back in 2013. I had spent the whole week thinking about how I was going to use the sermon to captivate and win souls for Christ.

I focused so much on the *how* that I lost sight of the *why*. Needless to say, that Saturday afternoon, I felt unprepared and fear crept into my heart, causing me to doubt that God was with me. The truth is, I was not prepared. I had not meditated nor did I spend time in prayer on behalf of the young people. I was eager to speak but had not been in the presence of God to actually hear God speak.

The spirit of fear can also come as a generational curse. It often produces anxiety, oversensitivity, and depression through generations. The roots of these spirits are rooted in disappointment, witchcraft, the sin of generations passed and personal sins. Because I grew up in a family that was not well off financially, I sometimes wondered if I would have to struggle like my parents did. I feared that I would end up not having enough to care for my family.

A good family friend one day expressed her fears to me when she revealed that she and her husband had filed for divorce. Oddly enough, her mother and grandmother both divorced at a young age. On the night of her honeymoon, she asked her husband how long he thought the marriage would last! She was fearful, and so the spirit of fear took over. As I began to speak to her, I quickly identified this as a generational pattern. Through prayer, she was able to denounce any ground that spirit had in her life. Many times, we spend time worrying about the things we cannot control. One thing we can control however is our relationship with our Savior. A true relationship with Christ will allow us to identify the spirit of fear. Once identified, it must be uprooted and cast out. One of the most exciting miracles done by Jesus was the healing of the man laying by the Bethesda pool. In the fifth chapter in the Book of John, Jesus went to the feast of Jews and decided to visit the pool of Bethesda. There laid a man who had an infirmity for thirty-eight years.

> When Jesus saw him lying there and learned that he had been in this condition for a long time, he asked him, "Do you want to get well?" "Sir," the invalid replied, "I have no one to help me into the pool when the water is stirred. While I am trying to get in, someone else goes down ahead of me." Then Jesus said to him, "Get up! Pick up your mat and walk." At once the man was cured; he picked up his mat and walked (John 5:6-9)

Once a year, it was said that an angel stirred up the waters and was believed that the first person to get in the pool would be healed of their infirmities. For almost his entire lifetime, this man was deemed paralyzed, invalid and a reject. His name is not even mentioned in the Bible. I can imagine how the side of the pool looked like and better yet, I can picture how this man felt and looked. I imagine that thousands flooded the side of the Pool of Bethesda waiting for this miracle to take place once a year. While laying helpless by the poolside, there came Jesus, in all of His Glory, questioning the man's desire for healing, "Do you want to get well?" He asked.

As soon as Jesus asked this question, the man began making excuses as to why he had not been healed. "Sir," the invalid replied, "I have no one to help me into the pool when the water is stirred. While I am trying to get in, someone else goes down ahead of me." This man, I presume, had no idea of the power that was in the Man who was standing beside him. He was so focused on his sickness that he lost sight of Jesus.

How many times do we complain and murmur about our desires that are taking longer to come to pass? Instead of acting on faith, we live in fear and never really get to live out our desires and dreams. The man I am sure felt helpless and desperate. However, his fear and lack of faith kept him bound to his sickness. He was too comfortable in his condition. In his heart, he knew he wanted the healing, but fear and the negativity surrounding him kept him stagnant.

Whether it is deliverance, healing, spiritual advancement, we have to want it so bad that we ban the naysayers, the negativity in our environments, and fear. When Jesus encountered the crippled man, He questioned the man's desire to get healed. Jesus said to him, "Stand up! Pick up your mat and walk." In other words, stop the complaining, stop the excuses and make a move! Just do it! That was it. Jesus healed the man in an instant.

Desire and faith go hand in hand. We can have the desire to be whatever we want, but if we lack faith, we might as well be sitting at the poolside just as the man was. It is easy for people to identify us based on our problems and issues. The woman with the issue of blood was identified just as that; one with an infirmity. No one knew her name, and no one cared. They knew her by her sickness. More often than not, we are headlined by our sicknesses, shortcomings, and sin.

In both cases, Jesus was ready to heal both the man by the poolside and the woman with the issue of blood. They, however, had to be ready to receive the healing. If they were not at the exact place and at the right time, they would have missed out on their deliverance. In a later chapter, we will touch on what happens when we align with the timing of God. God does not need a year, month, or even a day to turn things around for us. In fact, a million years to us is as a second to God. Whatever situation you are in right now, as long as there is life, it can be changed for the better.

As followers of Christ, we are not living by our own power or might, but by the power of the God. God has given each of us talents, spiritual and material gifts to use for His glory. Fear suppresses our spiritual gifts, and it minimizes our potential, making us feel as if we are not enough. It is time to say enough to fear. 2 Corinthians 12:9 says that God's grace is sufficient for every one of us and His strength is made perfect in our weakness.

What a relief it is to know that we are not in this battle alone! The great combination of power, love, and a sound mind is what will help us combat against fear. The world does not know what true love is. This kind of love is the *agape* love. It involves faithfulness, commitment, and an act of the will. This is God's love for us. He loves because that is His nature and the expression of His being. He loves the unlovable not because we deserve to be loved but because it is His nature to love. Once we understand this, it becomes easy to trust God and win the fight against the spirit of fear.

*Our mind is a battlefield, but God always wins.*

*Thank you, Lord, for your Word which brings a new revelation each time we read it. It equips us with the proper tools and understanding that we may withstand the evil darts of the enemy. God, I pray that you will reveal your secrets to me. Teach my hands to war, and my fingers to fight. Let your Spirit that has begun a great work; continue to prune me to your perfect will. In Jesus' Name I pray. Amen.*

"Finally, be strong in the Lord and in the strength of his might. Put on the whole armor of God that you may be able to stand against the schemes of the devil. For we do not wrestle against flesh and blood, but against the rulers, against the authorities, against the cosmic powers over this present darkness, against the spiritual forces of evil in the heavenly places."

*Ephesians 6:10-12*

# SPIRITUAL WARFARE

Behind every spirit, there is a deep-rooted history, and it is crucial for Christians not to live blindly to this fact. As Christians, the Spirit of God dwells in us, but the world as we know is filled with powers of influence that are demonic. These forces have existed since ancient times and have been fighting ever since to steal, kill, and destroy your life.

They have been trying since creation to increase and maintain their realms of power over regions and nations and your life. The reality is, Satan hates you and has a terrible plan for your life. If he cannot succeed in robbing you of eternal life, he will do everything in his power to deprive you of the peace, joy, and rewards that come from serving God in this life. Because of this, he has delegated much of his work to principalities, powers, and rulers in the heavenly realms to discourage, distract, and deceive through a variety of means. In John 12:31, Satan is referred to as the "ruler of this world."

It is reasonable to assume that Satan has some power, but is most certainly powerless before God because Christ has "disarmed principalities and powers, He made a public spectacle of them, triumphing over them" (Colossians 2:15). Many people tend to think that screaming, stomping, and shouting are required to defeat the devil, which is not at all true. The power of God is the only Force that can defeat the devil. The media has depicted the devil as this red little horned mystical figure running around with a fork. The sad reality is, Satan has sown disbelief in the hearts of millions, causing them not to believe he exists. The Bible provides abundant evidence to show that there are different levels in the spiritual realm. The kingdom of Satan is ranked and highly organized. Christians must not shun away from understanding how his system works. The devil has destroyed too many Christians who are ignorant of his devices and so we must be equipped, ready, and vigilant of his schemes.

In Daniel 10, the Bible speaks of fallen angels who ruled over several nations. Note that these 'princes' are not literal in the sense of human intellect. They are conniving; deceitful authority figures placed over regions and nations. Although these principalities have been assigned over these nations, God has given us all power and authority through His Son, Jesus Christ. By equipping ourselves with the Word of God, and wearing the correct gear as noted in Ephesians 6, we will be victorious.

It is crucial to understand that God has all authority and power over principals, powers, and demonic spirits. Colossians 1:16 tells us, "For in him all things were created: things in heaven and on earth, visible and invisible, whether thrones or powers or rulers or authorities; all things have been created through him and for him." If God is the creator of all things, He gives the commands needed for things to function. In the beginning, He spoke a word and said: "Let there be light," and there was light. In the same way, powers, principalities, and rulers are all under the authority of God and cannot function out of the will and beyond God's commands. This is proven by the dialogue which happened between Satan and God in the Book of Job. Satan had to ask permission to persecute Job.

From the least of them to the greatest, the entities that function in the kingdom of God are all under the submission of God's power.

In Ephesians 6:12, the apostle describes how Satan's kingdom has been militarily aligned. He writes, "For we wrestle not against flesh and blood, but against principalities, against powers, against the rulers of the darkness of this world, against spiritual wickedness in high places." The ranking system given here is in the ascending order from the earth. The lowest level are principalities, then powers, rulers of darkness and lastly, spiritual wickedness in high places.

The first group Paul mentions is principalities. The Greek definition of the word *principalities* is *archai* which denotes ancient time. Paul utilizes the word *principalities* to tell us that principalities have been assigned over the earth. It is important to note that principalities was actually the name assigned to a smaller state that was ruled by a prince or governor in a nation such as the Roman Empire. It is no surprise that these forces are the ones that Satan has assigned over regions or population. They are powerful evil beings that have held their haughty positions of power and authority since ancient times.

The second group Paul describes is "powers." Powers are those that hold power within a kingdom, a principality, or even an empire. The word *power* in Greek is translated as *exousia*. Powers have a jurisdiction of authority. They hold up prayers of the saints and fight against our prophetic words. In the book of Daniel, we see how a 'power' was assigned to delay and fight against the messenger of the Lord.

Daniel who went into a lengthy period of mourning, fasting and praying got his prayer delayed by the Prince of Persia. The messenger angel of the Lord told Daniel "but the prince of the Persian kingdom resisted me twenty-one days. Then Michael, one of the chief princes, came to help me, because I was detained there with the king of Persia" (Daniel 10:13). Powers have the ability to exert control, influence, creating and enforcing laws or authority over a people or nation.

They have been delegated power of influence from Satan in order to carry out all manner of evil in whichever ways they have been assigned. They are not as powerful as rulers in high places, but are stronger than principalities. These powers undoubtedly are behind heinous crimes against humanity, terrorism, gross poverty, sickness and disease, sex and drug abuse.

The highest level of the hierarchy is the spiritual wickedness in high places. These wicked spirits are dominating in the air (Ephesians 2:2). The word *wickedness* is taken from the word *poneros*, which is usually used to depict vicious or malevolent actions. These evil spirits are sent forth to viciously afflict humans.

There are thousands of demonic spirits lurking in the earth. Listed are some of the most common spirits that are running rampant in our churches today. They have in many ways hindered the spiritual, social, and economic advancement of Christians. When Christians are not aware that these spirits are manifesting, they live a distorted reality.

1. Spirit of control
2. Religious Spirit
3. Spirit of fear
4. Spirit of pride
5. Spirit of retaliation
6. Spirit of strife
7. Sexual impurity
8. Spirit of guilt
9. Occultism
10. Spirit of depression
11. Spirit of worry
12. Spirit of death

13. Spirit of poverty
14. Spirit of drunkenness
15. Spirit of perversion
16. Spirit of insecurity
17. Spirit of jealousy
18. Spirit of heaviness
19. Spirit of rejection
20. Spirit of Compromise

More often than not, churches fail to recognize the schemes and agenda of these spirits and have no plan to respond. In the Book of Hosea 4:6, the word of God says "my people perish for lack of knowledge." The lingering of these spirits in the church may cause congregational division, false teaching, the sheltering of sin, and discipleship distraction.

In order to be effective in spiritual warfare or our walk with Christ, we have to be *consistent* and *disciplined*. I will never forget the look one of the ladies at my local church gave me when I explained that God disliked lazy Christians. It is true that God loves us all, but He does not like our lack of prayer and discipline. Many have been programmed to accept latency in their spiritual lives. We each have to work to reach a higher glory in Christ. Authority is freely given, but we have to know the correct tactics in gaining such authority. We are more than conquerors through Jesus Christ, and nothing can ever change that. In the Book of Romans, Paul asks this question:

> "Who shall separate us from the love of Christ? Shall trouble or hardship or persecution or famine or nakedness or danger or sword? As it is written: "For your sake we face death all day long; we are considered as sheep to be slaughtered." No, in all these things we are more than conquerors through him who loved us. For I am convinced that neither death nor

life, neither angels nor demons, neither the present nor the future, nor any powers, neither height nor depth, nor anything else in all creation, will be able to separate us from the love of God that is in Christ Jesus our Lord."

(Romans 8:35-39)

We have an adversary, but we serve a greater and far more powerful God. Satan has no authority over our lives because we have been hidden under the powerful wings of God. The Psalmist David says it beautifully in Psalm 91, "He who dwells in the secret place of the Most High Shall abide under the shadow of the Almighty." This promise is not for everyone; it is for only those that *abide*. The word abide is linked to the Hebrew word, *katameno*, which means "constant residence."

God does not only want us to abide in Him only on Sunday mornings but rather wants us to be constantly joined with Him. He wants us to move and have our beings in Him. If we hide in God, the shadow of His wings will cover us because Satan and his evil host can do nothing the Lord does not allow them to do (Job 1-2).

Because the kingdom of darkness is highly organized, Satan uses several different devices to attack Christians. In her book, *How to Overcome Your Enemy*, Beena Philips, one of the greatest people I have encountered in the faith, gives seven main tactics the enemy uses to attack the church. I have provided these tactics and have taken a slight different approach in relating them to our walk with Christ. Below are listed some of the attacks of the enemy:

## Regression

The enemy causes people to go backward in their calls. Christians can go through spiritual, physical, social, and economic regression. Paul writes to Timothy and tells him that he has to fight a good fight to watch out to keep the faith and a good conscience. When focus is taken away from God, it can cause Christians to go in reverse in their lives.

## Repression

Repression, unlike regression, cannot always be identified or seen. Repression refers to the subconscious act of not acknowledging or acting upon one's feelings, thoughts, and wants. Repression is the act of bottling up or subduing our emotions and feelings. The enemy uses this tactic in our lives when we go through situations where we think "no one on earth could possibly relate to me, so I will keep this in without telling anyone." Spiritual oppression is subtle and can often go undiagnosed, though the symptoms are apparent for those who have the eyes to see exactly what is going on.

## Depression

Many people suffer from mental, or even spiritual, depression. Depression is a painful experience that is typically described with images of emptiness, darkness, heaviness, and even hell itself. David, a man after God's own heart, struggled greatly throughout his life with depression. In our churches today, we rub shoulders with people who are desperate, hurting, and lonely. To them, there is no way out of their current state. The enemy uses this tactic to attack the church with emptiness and heaviness. But just like David, God did not leave Him empty. He was by His side and comforted Him even through the toughest moments of his life. He can do the same for a hurting church.

## Oppression

Demonic oppression is when a demon is temporarily victorious over a Christian, successfully tempting a Christian to sin and hindering his ability to serve God with a strong testimony. If a Christian continues to allow demonic oppression in his/her life, the oppression can increase to the point that the demon has a very strong influence over the Christian's thoughts, behavior, and spirituality. For the Christian, the power for victory over and freedom from demonic oppression is always available. John declares, "The One who is in you is greater than the one who is in the world" (1 John 4:4). No demon, not even Satan himself, can prevent a Christian from surrendering to the Holy Spirit and thereby overcoming any demonic oppression.

## Obsession

Obsession is one of the most destructive characteristics a Christian can have. There are many different symptoms of obsession. Some Christians are obsessed with fear, money, fame, sex, lying, stealing, and even blaspheming against the Holy Spirit. Some Christians are even obsessed with religion that they have turned their hearts away from a true relationship with God! Through obsession, Demonic spirits can enter this way and take up residence in a home, a neighborhood, over a community, and even over a nation. The devil would love it if every Christian in the world were depressed because they would be easily defeated. 1 John 2:15-17 warns us to "not love the world or the things in the world. If anyone loves the world, the love of the Father is not in him. For all that is in the world—the desires of the flesh and the desires of the eyes and pride in possessions—is not from the Father but is from the world. And the world is passing away along with its desires, but whoever does the will of God abides forever."

## Possession

The Bible gives some examples of people possessed or influenced by demons. There is a distinct difference between being possessed by a demon and being oppressed or influenced by a demon. There is a wide variety of possible symptoms of demon possession, such as a physical impairment that cannot be attributed to an actual physiological problem, a personality change such as depression or aggression. While the Bible is clear that possession is real, it also unmistakably communicates the truth that God is sovereign over demons and that Jesus possesses full authority over the enemy. Surely, the Holy Spirit would not allow a demon to possess the same person He is indwelling. That is the reason it is crucial for Christians to dwell in the presence of God and be equipped with the power of God in order to withstand and resist the enemy.

> We must be vigilant and sharp in the spirit in order to identify the tactics of the enemy.

I find that in understanding the root of the spiritual world, there can be two dangers; underemphasis and overemphasis. God wants our attention to be on Him. He is a jealous God and wants our praise, worship, time, and energy. We should not be so focused on demonic activity that it takes our focus from the Creator, but we should not be oblivious to the fact that demonic activity exists.

Years ago, I attended a church who claimed they were Pentecostal and were functioning in the full authority of God. The people were so focused on spiritual warfare that the name of the Lord was rarely in their mouths. They had services almost every day of the week to fight against spiritual wickedness. Most of their 'worship' songs were not at all worship to God but rather seemed like some sort of a ritual. God was not pleased with the fact that so much focus was on the enemy and all of the Glory was taken from Him.

God wants us to be knowledgeable about the spiritual realm, but it is not His will for us to be consumed by these things. Our focus should always be on God as He alone is our help in trials.

The Hebrew word for "heavens" is *shamayim* and is in a plural form. From the Book of Genesis, the Bible speaks of three heavens— "In the beginning God created the Heavens and the earth" (Genesis 1:1). In its pluralistic form the word denotes that there is in fact more than one heaven.

Satan has been lurking the earth and has been *acting* like a lion, prowling, roaring and looking for someone to devour. The only true Lion is the Lion of Judah—Jesus Christ. He resurrected and had gone to prepare a place for every one of us. Because of the glory that waits, the devil has been working since the conception of time to deviate us from the Glory of God.

He has set up systems, ranks, and tactics to keep us from fulfilling our true purpose in Christ. In most of the churches, people are scared to speak about the tactics of the devil because they figure if they leave him alone, he will do the same. To be effective Christians, we must first know the power we have in our Lord Jesus Christ and how to effectively live in order to reach Heaven. A part of this is acknowledging that Satan is still at work today. From the moment you accept Jesus Christ as your personal Lord and Savior, there is a non-ending war for your soul. Many new converts, as well as Christians, who have long been in the faith, believe being a Christian ceases demonic attacks, struggles, and persecutions. In fact, for many, it intensifies. Ephesians 6 gives us the proper protocol and appropriate gear to advance and win this battle. To win the battle, we must know who we are fighting against.

The Bible is very particular and clear as to where Satan came from. His deceptive nature started since he swayed his fellow brethren, angels, bringing them into darkness. He lied to them, turning them against God.

"How art thou fallen from heaven, O Lucifer, son of the morning! How art thou cut down to the ground, which didst weaken the nations! For thou hast said in thine heart, I will ascend into heaven, I will exalt my throne above the stars of God: I will sit also upon the mount of the congregation, in the sides of the north: I will ascend above the heights of the clouds; I will be like the most High. Yet thou shalt be brought down to hell, to the sides of the pit." (Isaiah 14:12-17)

Satan is called many things. He is the accuser of the brethren as well as the adversary. He is the father of lies and works to destroy the children of God. He is full of pride, hate, and revenge. Satan rebelled against God and was cast out! In his fall from God's favor, he persuaded the angels of God and were casted out. These angels that were cast down are now doing earthly bindings and trying to stop the children of God from progressing in the Gospel of Christ. He has fought and plotted to even destroy the messianic line by tempting Jesus Christ (Matthew 4:1-11).

Not only is Satan the father of lies, but he also works overtime to blind the minds of unbelievers that they will not receive the salvation of the Lord. Paul, in the Book of 2 Corinthians 11, explains that Satan masquerades himself as an angel of light and righteousness. Satan presents sin to us as something pleasing and fulfilling. Unfortunately, even in churches today, he presents false teaching as enlightening and life-changing.

One of my good friends is a chaplain for the United States Army. In our conversations, he describes the organization of the military as one of the most complex and efficient structures in the world. Within the army, there are different ranks, groups, operational units, and tactics. A field army is different from a corps. A field army combines two or more corps with over fifty thousand soldiers and is usually led by a higher ranking officer. Besides the corps, there is a division which has about ten to sixteen thousand soldiers which are usually headed by a major general. From a division, the list goes down to a brigade which includes about 1,500 soldiers and is usually commanded by a colonel.

In the same way, the kingdom of Satan is arranged like an army. The satanic and demonic powers on earth are organized in hierarchies controlled by Satan. In Ephesians 6, Paul, by divine revelation, stated: "We wrestle not against flesh and blood, but against principalities, against powers, against the rulers of the darkness of this world, against spiritual wickedness in high places." We are given a profound description of the tactics and the organization of the kingdom of darkness. Continuing his description of Satan's military regime, he ranks the many forces.

Satan's purpose is to deceive nations and to keep people ignorant of God's truth and salvation through His Son, Jesus Christ. In the Book of Daniel, we see a spiritual battle fought by Michael, the archangel of God and the designated prince of Israel. A vision was communicated to Daniel: "Do not be afraid, Daniel. Since the first day that you set your mind to gain understanding and to humble yourself before your God, your words were heard, and I have come in response to them. But the prince of the Persian kingdom resisted me twenty-one days. Then Michael, one of the chief princes, came to help me, because I was detained there with the king of Persia" (Daniel 10: 12-13).

We can see that the battle was of such magnitude that Michael, the archangel of God assisted in the battle. Satan pursues and torments Christians so much because he knows that he has no future in the kingdom. In the Book of Revelation 20, Satan awaits the inevitable: he, along with all of the enemies of God, will be thrown into the lake of fire for all eternity. They will be tormented day and night forever and ever. His demise has not only been predicted, but it has been stamped and approved by our Lord and Savior. There will be no relief for Satan and the enemies of God. There will be eternal suffering and punishment for their sins against the infinitely holy God, whose wrath will be displayed forever.

*By equipping ourselves with the Word of God, and wearing the correct gear as noted in Ephesians six, we will be victorious.*

*God, I thank you because my identity is hidden in you. I have been crucified with Christ and through Him have gained access as an heir to the Kingdom of Heaven. Lord, in you I live, and in you I have my being. You truly are familiar with all of my ways. Because my identity is hidden in you, allow me the grace to live in holiness and righteousness that I may glory with Christ Jesus. In Jesus' name I pray. Amen.*

"You were taught, with regard to your former way of life, to put off your old self, which is being corrupted by its deceitful desires; to be made new in the attitude of your minds; and to put on the new self, created to be like God in true righteousness and holiness."

*Ephesians 4:22-25*

# FINDING SELF

According to Ephesians 2:10, we are God's greatest work of art. Yes, you! Now, you might be thinking, "Well, if God really knew my flaws, He probably would not think that," and that statement could not be further away from the truth. The reality is, every one of us was created in God's image and His perfect love is not based on our perfection, but His perfection. Once we have accepted our identity in Christ, we no longer chase after our fleshly desires but rather live by God's standards. By accepting this fact, we acknowledge that we are indeed living with Christ in Heavenly places.

Ephesians 1 tells us that we have been blessed with every spiritual blessing in Christ Jesus. Not only were we chosen from the foundations of the world, but we are redeemed and unconditionally loved and accepted. God sees us as blameless and pure through Jesus Christ. These aspects of our identity can never be altered by what we do, neither by our titles, our job descriptions nor by appearance.

It has become easier for us to identify with the world's terms of identity. With the rising age of the media, people are looking for more ways to feel validated and wanted. Social media, in particular, has created a broadcasting platform that amplifies feelings and invisibility. These things not only alter our perception, but they also provide a deranged image of our true identity and self-affirmation.

According to a research study done by *The common sense Census*, Americans spend about nine hours consuming media daily. That number quadrupled over the last decade. Time spent consuming music, reality shows, and movies have fueled the ongoing paranoia about who we should be and how we should live our lives. The average person will spend about five years and four months on social media over a lifetime. Media not only influences us mentally, but it also can have a negative effect spiritually. It heightens our sense to feel superior and impacts how we view our bodies compared to others and can also influence risky behaviors such as drinking alcohol, sexual misconduct, and taking of drugs.

Many Christians are having an identity crisis and are using mega-doses of self-affirmation as the cure. Few use the media to share the good news of our Lord Jesus Christ. Teenagers, in particular, are deliberately captivated through magazines, television shows, music videos, and apps. Everything is at the tip of our fingers.

---

## We are redeemed, unconditionally loved and accepted

---

Timelines are filled with live reactions and raw emotions. Opinions are drawn like swords while carnality gets the best of us. We get lost in all of the movement and sometimes confuse our identity and reality for a fairytale and lies. The flesh loves validation and what a better place for the flesh to come alive than on social media? James tells us that "Each one is tempted when he is carried away and enticed by his own lust" (James 1:14).

In the Book of 1 John, the Bible pleads with us not to love the world or anything in the world. If anyone loves the world, the love for the Father is not in them. At the heart of this identity crisis are "the lust of the flesh, the lust of the eyes, and the pride of life—which comes not from the Father but from the world" (1 John 2:15-17).

Comparing our daily lives and judging the decisions others make can suck the life right out of us. Yet, daily, we spend hours comparing, judging, analyzing each other. In many facets, we have chosen man over God. We often impose our personal convictions on others as if we are more holy than they are. Our identity is not our profession, it is not our job or career, nor is it our social and economic status. We have gotten so used to the temporary situations that we face that some have even used those terms as identifiers for themselves.

---

## Our identity is not our profession.

---

A couple of years ago, I was at the supermarket and had bumped into a long lost acquaintance. Upon speaking to her, she began to describe herself as divorced and bankrupt. She was missing the mark! It is true that these situations can leave a lasting impact on our lives, but they are not our identity. We are far bigger than the circumstances we face on this earth.

Every year, I host a business conference where people come from all walks of life to showcase their business and speak about their successes and failures. So often, people would come up and introduce themselves as salesmen or accountants. One young lady, in particular, left a lasting impression. When introducing herself, she mentioned she was not a businesswoman but rather was in search of her true purpose and identity. She was not sure what avenue or career she wanted to go into. I began to speak to her about her passion and moreover, what God thinks of her true identity.

For years, she felt a strong pull to teach. Following her mother's footsteps, however, she landed a job at a tax firm but never felt fulfilled. Upon speaking to her about her passion for teaching, she began to feel connected to a higher call to serve. She had allowed all the chatter around her to cease and had now given way to the Holy Spirit to lead her. Now, she is thriving as a teacher at Somerville's school district.

Most keep their identification in their back pockets. But if I were to ask, who are you—what would your answer be? Would your answer be based on your wealth, career, and passion, or would it be according to your identity in Christ? Matter of fact, who are you in Christ? Are people able to identify the light in you? Many Christians in the United States are suffering from loss of identity. They simply do not know who they are and even more critical—whose they are.

In our corporate world, we have been programmed to express or think of our identity based on the nature of our jobs, careers, and sometimes, even our sins. Apostle Paul, in a letter to the Galatians, writes: "I am crucified with Christ: nevertheless I live; yet not I, but Christ liveth in me" (Galatians 2:20). Many times, in the Bible, there is a plea for Christians to put away the 'old carnal man' and to be joined with Christ who is the truth, the way, and the life.

Christians have worked so hard to live up to the expectation of their daily lifestyles that sometimes, our identity in Christ is hidden. We compromise to worldly standards in order to make those of the world feel more comfortable. Once those standards are no longer applicable, the very foundation of our identity is shaken and altered.

Beautiful things happen when we allow God to mold our identity to His perfect will. The word *psuché* is the Greek word for breath or soul. According to the Old Testament, the soul is the direct aftermath of God's breathing. In order to live out of the fullness of our identity in Christ, we must determine the things that may hinder us from doing so. Some hindrances may be sin, emotions, lack of a prayer life, and most importantly, denying the Salvation of the Lord.

God wants us to prosper in all aspects; however, our salvation is worth more than the car, house, job, and even the husband or wife. Because the enemy knows we have the desire for these things, he keeps us entertained and busy in trying to gain these self-fulfilling things, while forsaking the true Gospel. Sin is the attitude and subsequent action that separates us from God and each other. It is no doubt that Satan's greatest threat to any of us is a permanent separation from God. Temptations are everywhere, and the flesh is weak. It is important to know that God already gave us the victory through His Son, Jesus Christ. We must enter the battlefield readily armed and equipped with the word of God. Christ disarmed the powers of Satan and already destroyed sin. The enemy is working double time and overtime to see how he can reverse and cancel what was already accomplished on the Cross. Sin tarnishes our identity and always leads us astray.

The word is describes in the Bible as transgression of the law of God (1 John 3:4). John writes "Everyone who makes a practice of sinning also practices lawlessness; sin is lawlessness." We are all sinners, even those who have been saved as Paul says "all have sinned and fall short of the glory of God" (Romans 3:23). Sin separates us from God and causes us to feel empty and void. Isaiah writes "your iniquities have made a separation between you and your God, and your sins have hidden his face from you so that he does not hear" (Isaiah 59:2). Sin is rooted in the fall of Lucifer, not content with his position; he desired to be higher than God, which caused him to be banned from Heaven. Bringing sin to the human race, he tempted Adam and Eve with enticement which caused them to rebel against God.

Just like he had done, he wanted the human race to think that they were higher than God. In Genesis 3, the sycophantic serpent lured Eve by asking "did God actually say, 'You shall not eat of any tree in the garden?" He knew from the beginning that his plan was to see the fall of man. Satan knows the plans that God has in store for your life and that is why he has been working so hard to infiltrate your mind, your heart and your life.

The main tool the enemy uses against the people of God is undoubtedly sin. Once we lose ourselves to sin, we lose our identity. The word itself derives from the Greek word *harmatia* which means "misses the mark" (in the way an archer's arrow misses the mark). Sin is hostile to our well-being and seeks dominion over us and our world. Its ultimate purpose is to bring death and its aim is to destroy us. Our love story with Christ however starts with his love for us, not vile nature of sin. The inherent inclination to sin entered the human race through Adam. Since then, human beings became sinners by nature. When Adam sinned, his inner nature was transformed by his rebellion, bringing to him spiritual death and depravity which would be passed on to all who came after him. The Bible is clear that we cannot serve two masters at once. The power of the Cross overcame the power of sin, but we have to make the conscious decision to abide in this truth. In the First Epistle of John, we read;

> "No one who abides in him keeps on sinning; no one who keeps on sinning has either seen him or known him. Little children, let no one deceive you. Whoever practices righteousness is righteous, as he is righteous. Whoever makes a practice of sinning is of the devil, for the devil has been sinning from the beginning. The reason the Son of God appeared was to destroy the works of the devil. No one born of God makes a practice of sinning, for God's seed abides in him, and he cannot keep on sinning because he has been born of God. By this it is evident who are the children of God, and who are the children of the devil: whoever does not practice righteousness is not of God, nor is the one who does not love his brother." (1 John 3:6-10)

In the words of Sinach, a Nigerian Gospel singer, "We are a chosen generation, called forth to show God's excellence." Everything we need to prosper, God has provided and has built in us. From the beginning, God has made known to us what is right from wrong. To Adam in the Garden, God said, "You are free to eat from any tree in the garden; but you must not eat from the tree of the knowledge of good and evil, for when you eat of it you will surely die" (Genesis 2:16-17). In the book of Exodus, God carves out His desires and laws for the people of Israel; From the Ten Commandments we have false worship, idolatry, misusing God's name, violating the Sabbath, dishonoring parents, murder, adultery, stealing, lying/libel, and coveting. God never leaves us ignorant of His desires for us pertaining to our salvation. He gives us the blueprint and has reinforced His divine desire for us to be saved through His son Jesus Christ. Anyone who chooses to live in sin will not inherit the Kingdom of Heaven.

All wrongdoing is sin and when we are compelled to commit these acts, we should be reminded of the harsh reality that our eternity with Christ in in jeopardy every time we sin. He has given us a diverse set of tools to help us prosper in all aspects. This generation has been fed the Word of God at every angle. One of our main issues is not that we lack the knowledge of who God is but rather our lack of *order* and *discipline*. We have been taught how to live righteously, how to pray, and how to read the word. Still, many Christians are oblivious to the tactics of the enemy. How can we fight well when we have no idea what we are up against?

That is the reason why, in this great love story, God's love wins, every single time. As Christians, we are inherently spiritual beings who thrive and flourish when we attach and become one with God. Sin in its full nature is to separate and to alienate us from the will of God. Apostle Paul makes certain of this by stating that "if anyone is in Christ, he is a new creation. The old has passed away; behold, the new has come" (2 Corinthians 5:17). Our relationship with God should not be second resort and should not be optional. It is a requirement to our salvation.

God hates sin because He is a Holy God. The Bible presents God's attitude toward sin with strong feelings of hostility, disgust, and utter dislike. God hates sin because sin separates us from Him and tears us of our true identity which can only be found in God. The continual sins in our lives "have separated [us] from your God; [our] sins have hidden His face from [us], so that He will not hear" (Isaiah 59:2).

The Christian walk is a continuous process of gradual change and growth and when we sin, we not only damage ourselves, but also those around us. Sinning violates our inclinations and needs because we are denying the very things that are good for us. Over my years in ministry, I have encountered some who think their strong commitment to their local church, whether financially or through works, will allow them good standing with God. It is by Grace we have been saved, this is not a work of ourselves but really is a gift from God. Grace is an unmerited favor but does not give us the right to sin against God. We should not nullify the law because of Grace but rather should live our lives to uphold the commandments of God.

Finding our identity in Christ is finding the confidence in Him to know we are enough to say no to sin and to live righteously. No longer do we need to find our worth in external circumstances because we are hidden in Christ Jesus, the author, and finisher of our faith.

*We are Grace-lavished!*

*Dear Heavenly Father, I pray for the virtue of patience in my life and the lives of everyone around me. I pray that your peace will live in my heart when I feel discouraged, in despair, and afraid. Help me to understand that my waiting place is a growing place. Help me to understand that the pressures of this life are meant to build my character so that I may understand my potential in you. In Jesus' Name I pray. Amen*

More than that, we rejoice in our sufferings, knowing that suffering produces endurance, and endurance produces character, and character produces hope

*Romans 5:3-5*

# THE WAITING PLACE

Waiting perhaps is one of the hardest things we can ever do, especially when God has called us to a particular mission. With each mission, however, comes the perfect season. Waiting not only tests our patience but it strengthens our character in Christ. God has a way of keeping us in the process longer than we have in mind. In those moments, He works to refine our spirits, align us with His purpose and drive us towards our destiny. I like to think the promises of God consist of two main categories; the timing and the placement. Each one of us has the potential to fulfill our callings according to the perfect will of God. By aligning ourselves with the right timing and placement of God, He is able to use our waiting period as a catalyst for our spiritual, financial, social and all-around wellness.

We all want good things to happen in our lives, but we seldom plan for disappointments, detours, heartaches, and all of the sadness that are often presented. When these things happen in our lives, they steal our joy, take away our focus, and can leave us feeling hopeless. Although it is a tough place to be, every one of us has or will someday experience the *waiting place*. The good news is God will never leave you in the wait alone. He says in Isaiah 41:40, "Fear not, for I am with you; be not dismayed, for I am your God; I will strengthen you, I will help you, I will uphold you with my righteous right hand." God is aware of your waiting place. He has not overlooked your process nor has he forgotten you there.

One of my favorite Biblical stories is that of the three Hebrew boys: Shadrach, Meshach, and Abed-Nego. The Scriptures vividly displays the journey of these young men as they went through captivity in the land of Babylon. In the Book of Daniel, the three young boys are introduced to us as the young men that refused to bow down to the king's image. King Nebuchadnezzar set up a golden image and demanded that all of the people of the land worshiped the idol. Everyone who disobeyed with this decree would have the consequence of death.

The three men refused, stating, "King Nebuchadnezzar, we do not need to defend ourselves before you in this matter. If we are thrown into the blazing furnace, the God we serve is able to deliver us from it, and he will deliver us from Your Majesty's hand. But even if he does not, we want you to know, Your Majesty, that we will not serve your gods or worship the image of gold you have set up" (Daniel 3:15-18). Now, that is boldness! They stood firm in their decision not to idolize the false god of the land. They made up in their minds and spirits that they would not bow down to any other God but The True Living God.

But like us, the three Hebrew boys had to go through a process. First, they were put under *pressure*. It is amazing what some pressure will do to us. The saying that diamonds are made in the rough is true to every Christian.

The diamond is the hardest of all gemstones known to man, yet it is composed of only one element—common carbon. As simple as its make up is, it goes through some extreme pressure and heat before it can actually become a refined diamond. God, sometimes, in our wait, allow circumstances to happen so that they shape our view of who He is. If we never go through pain, we will not understand that

72

there is a healer who heals. If we never go through the heartaches, confusion, and despair, we will never know God as the loving counselor that He is.

Shadrach, Meshach, and Abed-Nego, upon their capture, knew in their hearts that the season they had entered into was going to be defying. Yet, instead of running away from the pressure, they pursued on with boldness by looking at the issue straight on.

You might be going through a situation right now that is testing your patience or character. It may be that you are waiting on your husband or wife and you've poured your heart out to God, but still, no one to show for it. I remember before I was married, I went through a long period of waiting and pressure. I was praying for God to reveal His will regarding my life partner. After having gone through the heartbreaks and hurt, I knew that God was the only one that could restore and align me with my husband and so, I decided to wait.

You might be going through a season of financial drought and are waiting for God to show up and provide. Keep in mind that God is Jehovah Jireh; the Lord who provides. In Genesis 22, God provided for Abraham after asking him to make a sacrificial offering.

By testing Abraham's obedience, He asked Him to offer his son, Isaac. Although Abraham was probably frightened and shaken by this request, he obeyed God. God had other plans; He instead offered a lamb for the sacrifice.

---

The wait is not meant to kill you; it is
meant to strengthen you.

---

The waiting place is difficult as it requires sacrifice, attentiveness, and faith. The wait is not meant to kill you but is meant to strengthen you for the glory that awaits. Maybe you are waiting on the doctor's diagnosis or a solution for a family issue. Perhaps you have prayed, begged, or even pleaded with God over something that is dear to your heart. Each one of us is at a different mark in our wait. Some are closer to the finish line, and others have just started. In all circumstances, however, we must remind ourselves that God is Sovereign and makes no mistakes.

In Proverbs 3:5-6, it urges us to "trust in the LORD with all [our] heart and lean not on [our] own understanding; in all [our] ways submit to him, and he will make [our] paths straight." God is the finisher of our faith, and so we must trust that His plans are perfect for us, even if we do not know what is going on. Sometimes, God takes us through a waiting period so that we may let go of our human expectations and cling to His promises. David said: "I waited patiently for the Lord; he turned to me and heard my cry. He lifted me out of the slimy pit, out of the mud and mire; he set my feet on a rock and gave me a firm place to stand. He put a new song in my mouth, a hymn of praise to our God. Many will see and fear the Lord and put their trust in him" (Psalm 42:1-3). If God did this for David, He can surely do it for you. God is no respecter of persons. For us to wait effectively, there are some principles we must follow. First, while waiting, we must wait actively. One of my friends began to worry as she waited for her husband. The issue was, she never went out, never visited new places and to put it nicely, hated the idea of being around unfamiliar faces. Several times, I would advise her to go out and meet new people. She refused. Someone like this, praying could help other things, but God will not do your part! Besides, faith without works is dead.

Secondly, we have to make up our minds that our focus will not be on the circumstances, but rather will be fixed on Jesus Himself. So many things grapple our attention. We can get lost in the wait if we allow our attention to be on everything else but God. Lastly, we have to be strong and courageous. I've found that one of my biggest battles in long seasons of waiting is fighting fear and worry. A voice in my head asks, What if this happens? What if God doesn't answer your prayers? What if this goes wrong? In those times, the Holy Spirit quickly reminds me that God is omniscient and omnipotent. He sees and knows all things. Nothing can hide from the presence of God.

God is with you wherever you go, and He will never leave your side. The enemy wants us to think in our waiting season that we are alone; that is a lie from the father of lies. In fact, "The angels of the Lord encamp around those who fear Him, to deliver them out of danger" (Psalm 34). If you could see into the spiritual realm, you would see angels who are standing by your side, waiting for commands to carry out on your behalf! You are not alone and should not feel as though you are. The wait may be long, but those who endure in the wait will reap the promise.

The enemy has a way of anticipating your reaction to the delays, detours, and reroutes. This is the reason he sometimes rushes our process by providing the wrong promise. He does this often when we do not allow ourselves to wait on the promises of the Lord. The devil even tempted Jesus by providing a way out of His fast. In Matthew 4:1, we see this interaction;

> "Then Jesus was led up by the Spirit into the wilderness to be tempted by the devil. And when He had fasted forty days and forty nights, afterward He was hungry. Now when the tempter came to Him, he said, "If You are the Son of God, command that these stones become bread. But He answered and said, "It is written, 'Man shall not live by bread alone, but by every word that proceeds from the mouth of God."

Satan and its hosts a way of manipulating facts, displaying them as distorted reality, to trick Christians out of their true promise. Of course, if Jesus wanted, He could have turned the stones into bread, but He knew His mission and most importantly, kept His focus on God—The Bread of Life.

Years ago, I was introduced to a person who clearly had been called by God. When the man preached, he preached with the fire of the Holy Spirit, and people came to know Jesus through him. A couple of years ago, he was found dead in his hotel room on a drug overdose. In conversation leading up to his death, his pastor revealed that he had gone through a long period where he felt hopeless about the prophetic words that had been released in his life. Early in his life, prophetic words were released in his life which indicated that his ministry would bloom all across the country and that if he stayed the course, his ministry would reach thousands.

For years, the man held on to the promise of the word but not to the One who gave him the promise. He envied so much to preach at mega churches that he forgot the mission God gave him to accomplish at local churches. Sometimes, words are spoken over our lives to test our understanding of who God is. We must not idolize prophetic words so much that we forget about the mission of the word itself. Our ministries, gifts, and talents are for the benefit of the church— not for our selfish personal desires and gain. Sure, we can be blessed through those things, but our motivation should not solely be for materialistic blessings.

---

The enemy sometimes rushes our process by providing the wrong promise.

---

Satan sowed seeds of hopelessness into his heart and made him feel like his works in the kingdom were void. He started to find other outlets to let out his frustration, and eventually, turned to drugs. He was still preaching and ministering, yet

God did not know him. Someone once said God is the only one that can fire you and keep you employed at the same time. Though he could preach and minister to others, he was living out of the promise. Although the prophetic words given were of great promise and purpose, Satan created a distorted reality for him, causing him to envy fame and power over the prize of heaven. This is a pure example of why we must know *who* we are in Christ and most importantly, *whose* we are. Understanding these things will allow us to wait it out during our toughest seasons.

As it says in the Book of Habakkuk 2:3, "For the revelation awaits an appointed time; it speaks of the end and will not prove false. Though it linger, wait for it; it will certainly come and will not delay." Every prophetic word that has ever been spoken over our life awaits its appointed time. Many times, those words are conditional and require great work on our end as well. Knowing who our Father is and what His word says about us will give us that no matter the length of the wait, no matter the detours and reroutes, we will make it; with the condition that we keep our eyes on God. Waiting on God is greatly associated with the blessings of God. One of the most tested men in the Old Testament is Job. To prove his faithfulness to the Lord, God allowed the devil to destroy everything he had. He was tested physically, mentally, socially, and spiritually. Job was not an ordinary man. In fact, according to Job 1, he was blameless and upright. Not only that, he feared God and shunned evil. The Bible even goes as far as to say that "he was the greatest man among all the people of the East" (Job 1:3). He had character, wealth, health, and a large family. All was going well with Job until the devil, the accuser of the brethren came to God, asking for permission to persecute Job.

God from heaven bragged on Job's faithfulness to Him— this, of course, bothered Satan. Wanting to truly test Job's faithfulness to God, Satan said: "Have you not put a hedge around him and his household and everything he has? You have blessed the work of his hands, so that his flocks and herds are spread throughout the land. But now stretch out your hand and strike everything he has, and he will surely curse you to your face" (Job 1:9-11). God, however, wanted to prove that Job was not righteous simply because of his riches and blessings, and permitted Satan to test Job. Isn't it amazing that the power of Satan is actually in the hands of God? Without permission, he cannot touch you and his power (or lack thereof) is powerless!

God challenged the devil telling him, "Very well, then, everything he has is in your power, but on the man himself do not lay a finger" (Job 1:12). Job lost just about everything; his sheep, his oxen, his camels, his servants, and all of his sons and daughters. One thing he did not lose was his faith in God. The Bible tells us "then Job arose, tore his robe, and shaved his head; and he fell to the ground and worshiped. And he said: "Naked I came from my mother's womb, and naked shall I return there. The LORD gave, and the LORD has taken away; Blessed be the name of the LORD. In its entirety, Job did not sin nor charge God with wrong" (Job 1:20-22). How powerful is that! Imagine having everything you care about taken and stripped away; your health, family, job, friends, and life partner.

What would your reaction be towards God? Maybe you have been in a place where something dear to you has been taken away. Perhaps you are at a place where you've been questioning God about the reasoning behind the hurts, pains, confusion, and loss. Is your faith in this time strong enough to withstand the trying times?

The story of Job did not end there. God has a way of showing up and showing off for His children. After the persecution came greater reward. Job 42:10-17 tells us;

"After Job had prayed for his friends, the LORD restored his prosperity and doubled his [previous] possessions. All his brothers, sisters, and former acquaintances came to his house and dined with him in his house. They offered him sympathy and comfort concerning all the adversity the LORD had brought on him. Each one gave him a qesitah and a gold earring. So the LORD blessed the latter part of Job's life more than the earlier. He owned 14,000 sheep, 6,000 camels, 1,000 yoke of oxen, and 1,000 female donkeys. He also had seven sons and three daughters. He named his first [daughter] Jemimah, his second Keziah, and his third Keren-happuch. No women as beautiful as Job's daughters could be found in all the land and their father granted them an inheritance with their brothers. Job lived 140 years after this and saw his children and their children to the fourth generation. Then Job died, old and full of days."

God blessed Job double for his trouble! He reaped a far greater reward than he had prior to the persecution. In the same way, Christians in this life will be tried and tested. God gives us a command in 1 Peter 4:12-13, telling us to "not be surprised at the fiery trial when it comes upon [us] to test [us], as though something strange were happening to [us]. But rejoice insofar as [we] share Christ's sufferings, that [we] may also rejoice and be glad when his glory is revealed."

Matthew, a great Apostle of the Lord, expanded on this by reassuring us, "Blessed are those who are persecuted because of righteousness, for theirs is the kingdom of heaven" (Matthew 5:10). The Kingdom of Heaven is for you to gain but there is a hell to avoid. In our moments of waiting on God, we should be focused and in tune with the voice of God. Our faith should never waver because of the things we lose in this world because to lose for the sake of Jesus Christ is to gain. As we wait on our Heavenly reward, we should be hopeful in the Glory that awaits us in Christ Jesus.

*After the persecution comes a far greater reward.*

*Father, I come before you now, and I surrender all that I am to you. I acknowledge that before the foundation of the world, you knew me and in your pursuit of me, you sent your Son to die on Calvary. Lord, I want to seek you like never before. My soul thirsts after you. Teach me the way to your heart that I may draw near to you. In Jesus' Name I pray. Amen.*

"For I am convinced that neither death nor life, neither angels nor demons, neither the present nor the future, nor any powers, neither height nor depth, nor anything else in all creation, will be able to separate us from the love of God that is in Christ Jesus our Lord."

*Romans 8:38-39*

# GOD'S PURSUITS

Man was created with a set purpose, plan, and for the Glory of God. Moreover, God has purposely sought us since creation. No other being, whether celestial or terrestrial was made in the likeness of God. We are intricately designed, and even our soul knows this well according to Psalm 34. Contrary to worldly beliefs, the origin of man is not of natural evolution or from atom theory but rather conceived from the mind of God. From the beginning of creation, God reveals Himself as One who is seeking communion with mankind. In Genesis 3, we see God graciously seeking the guilty sinners, and providing a way to restoration. God's *agape* love is shown for us at the cross. This type of love is not a sappy, sentimental feeling such as we often portray. God's love is unconditional, and unchanging.

When sin entered the heart of man, they stepped out of the perfect will of God and were lost in reference to God. Through Adam, the inherent inclination to sin entered our hearts, causing humankind to become sinners by nature. Through the Grace of God, however, we have been redeemed as sons and daughters of Christ. We are not valuable to God because of any great works we have done, but God values us simply because we exist. His purpose for us is to know Him and to be like He is. In 1 John 1:5-7, we see that God is light—in fact; He is *the* light, which is why, "If we say we have fellowship with him while we walk in darkness, we lie and do not practice the truth. But if we walk in the light, as he is in the light, we have fellowship with one another, and the blood of Jesus his Son cleanses us from all sin."

Sin always leads to guilt, shame, and alienation. It isolates us from the face of God and with others. After having disobeyed the Lord's instructions, Adam and Eve hid from the Lord among the trees of the garden. Instead of starting over with creation, God looked for Adam and Eve, 'Where are you?' He cried out in the garden. Even though they stepped out of God's divine will, He sought them because His love for us surpasses our transgressions.

The life we live should help paint a picture of who God is. Sometimes, we fall short of that painting; I know I do. Although we deserve judgment, God is not stoic but rather patient and desires for us to be saved. How many times have we disobeyed, fallen short, or have stepped out of His perfect will? According to Romans 3:23, all have sinned and have fallen short of the Glory of God. Although God is patient with us to repent and to live as light, the gifts He has placed inside of us suffer when we chose to stay in the filth of sin.

As explained in an earlier chapter, sin comes from the Greek word *hamartia*, which means "missed the mark." Beyond its ability to keep those who are bound by it tangled with the desires of the flesh, it consumes and dries up purpose and one's destiny. It not only quenches our joy, but it also robs us of confidence in prayer and causes anguish in our hearts. But why am I talking about sin if this chapter is called "God's Pursuit"? I speak on this because "without the shedding of blood, there is no forgiveness of sins" (Hebrews 9:22).

---

I was running from God, but His
grace outran my efforts.

---

For years, I had a personal sin that took over my life. It suffocated and veiled my calling to preach the Gospel and step into my Prophetic Grace. Even in the mess, God pursued my heart. He wanted me to know that my fleshly desires could never satisfy the lonely person I was. I was running from God, but His grace outran my efforts. No matter how unclean, ashamed, or unworthy I felt, He continually pursued me through His Word, His servants, and personal revelation. Early in my ministry, God used several different ministers, prophets, and pastors to confirm my calling.

I remember one particular night I was invited to attend a prophetic conference with my sister. Reluctant to attend, I decided to go. While there, the Holy Spirit revealed and confirmed my exact thoughts and ministry. For the years to follow, He continually did so. It was that night that the veil began to come off my ministry. I started walking boldly in my Prophetic Grace because I knew God's pursuit was nothing short of extraordinary.

King David, after his sin of murder and adultery, asked God to restore to him the joy of God's salvation, and for him to be upheld in God's generous Spirit. The Spirit of God convicts us of our sins that we may turn to God for restoration. It is through the precious blood of Christ that we have the right to such restoration and redemption. Once we have accepted Christ into our lives, He forgives us as far as the east is from the west. Though this came with the price of the cross, Jesus bore our sins, and now we are free.

---

You are valuable to God simply
because you exist

---

I know a young lady who spent years praying for healing from a very rare disease. She was following the routine protocol of church and thought she checked all the marks to have a *Christian* life. She attended church every Sunday and was part of the choir at church. Occasionally, she would even volunteer at the Bible Study class. Why was she not getting the results she prayed for? One day, she asked me to pray with her, and by the leading of the Holy Spirit, I asked her to begin the prayer session. She immediately started praying by asking God to heal her from the disease. There was no moment of confession or conversation with God.

A problem many Christians have is that they treat God as a wish box. Some say, *"Maybe, just maybe if I work hard enough, God will see me and will answer my prayers."* This couldn't be further away from the truth. According to Ephesians 2:8-9, it is by grace you and I have been saved through faith—and this is not from ourselves, it is the gift of God! Our salvation is not dependent on how many times you swept the church or how many times you volunteered at the thrift shop down the street. Sure, these things matter, but it is only through faith in Jesus Christ we can be healed, delivered, and set free!

After the prayer, I felt heavily on my heart to tell her that one of the reasons she was still sick was because of a particular sin she commits daily—the following of astrology. I began to speak to her about the implications this sin has on her life. She could not believe that God would reveal such a thing.

Immediately, the young lady began to pour out her heart to God, confessing her sin and asking for forgiveness. It was not more than two months; she was miraculously cured of the disease. In my follow-up conversation with her, she explained that for years, she was involved in astrology readings. Every time she had those readings, she would feel ashamed, lonely, and the sickness worsened.

God was tugging at her heart and had deliberately spoken to her about repentance. Out of stubbornness, she rebelled. Several times a year, she would go to church revivals and would hear the word and would get excited. As soon as she gets home, she would start reading astrology. She had a likeness of light, but in reality, did not know the light.

After years of living in denial and with this sin, she was tired and asked God to reveal to her what was holding her captive to this disease. I did not know this was a prayer she prayed a couple of days prior to asking me to pray with her. God is a just God and will provide a way for us to flee temptation. It is God's will that we reign in glory with Christ. He pursued the heart of the young lady through personal prophecy and word of knowledge.

Sin is in the very human nature of man, but upon acceptance of Jesus Christ as our personal Lord and Savior, we transform as ambassadors for the kingdom of God and must live as so. In fact, "no temptation has overtaken us except what is common to mankind. And God is faithful; he will not let us be tempted beyond what we can bear" (1 Corinthians 10:13). Grace, however, does not mean we are freed to do whatever we please. In fact, once we accept Jesus Christ as our Lord and Savior, we are now slaves to righteousness and not to sin. The devil has a way of pinning us in a corner to make us feel unworthy. Each one of us will appear before the judgment seat, but we should not fear for the moment when we do. As followers of Christ, sin should not become a lifestyle. It should be dealt with severely until it dissipates.

From the beginning of time, Satan has always been the accuser of the brethren. At every turn, he tries to convince us that God does not love us and that our sins are far too much to be forgiven. Those thoughts are lies and are from the father of lies—the devil. When responding to God's pursuit, we have to remember only what He says about us which can only be found in God's Holy Word.

Towards the end of His earthly ministry, Jesus pleaded to God for our sake, "Father, I want those you have given me to be with me where I am, and to see my glory, the glory you have given me because you loved me before the creation of the world" (John 17:24). Psalm 139 affirms this pursuit by painting a portrait of God's love for us: "You have searched me, Lord, and you know me. You know when I sit and when I rise; you perceive my thoughts from afar. You discern my going out and my lying down; you are familiar with all my ways. Before a word is on my tongue you, Lord, know it completely" (Psalm 139: 1-4). God is omnipresent, omniscience, and omnipotent. He is everywhere, knows everything and is all-powerful. We cannot hide from Him, neither can our sins, shortcomings, temptations or deepest darkest secrets. Before you were born, God foreknew you and created you purposefully for His divine will.

---

## God's pursuit is personal to every one of us.

---

One of the most powerful revelations one can have in their walk with Christ is to realize that God began the pursuit. God's pursuit is personal to every one of us and no sin is too big to keep Him away from us. One of my favorite love letters is found in the Book of Romans 8: 38-39: "For I am convinced that neither death nor life, neither angels nor demons, neither the present nor the future, nor any powers neither height nor depth, nor anything else in all creation, will be able to separate us from the love of God that is in Christ Jesus our Lord." What an assurance we have in Christ!

Recently, as I was reading the Word, a horrible thought began to formulate in my mind. It was not surprising that the thoughts came—what surprised me the most was how quickly God responded to the attack. As the thoughts began to unravel, the Holy Spirit quickly began to remind me of the endurance and perseverance Jesus had when the devil tempted Him not once, not twice, but three times in Matthew 4:

Then Jesus was led by the Spirit into the wilderness to be tempted by the devil. After fasting forty days and forty nights, he was hungry. The tempter came to him and said, "if you are the son of God, tell these stones to become Bread." Jesus answered, "It is written: Man Shall not live on Bread alone but on every word that comes from the mouth of God."

Surely, that passage brought revelation to my spirit on the promises of God unto us. The word of God says in 1 Corinthians 10:13: "No temptation has overtaken you except what is common to mankind." It is interesting to know that the "temptations" we go through are very common to everyone else out there. You are not the only one going through it! One way the devil attacks us is, after projecting the thoughts in our minds, he tries to blame us by making us feel like we're dirty, not worthy, and that we are the only ones battling against certain thoughts, situations, and emotions. That is a complete LIE! One of the ways we self-destruct is through our thought patterns. In effect, the devil works to attack the mind of the believer by giving the illusion that the temptations we face alienate us from the world.

Ever wonder why suicide rates have skyrocketed in the past decade? Ever wonder why more and more teens are now turning to drugs and alcohol just to "feel like themselves"? It's all the work of the enemy. He knows if he can attack your mind, he can surely attack your life, your purpose, and can eventually lead you to hell.

The next part of the verse (1 Corinthian 10:13) spoke to me the loudest. God Himself says, "He will not let [us] be tempted beyond what we can bear. But when [we] are tempted, He will also provide a way out so that [we] can endure." God knows our human nature so well (after all He did create us), that He personally created a way out of the temptations we may face.

James explains this perfectly in the Book of James, the first chapter by saying, "Consider it pure joy my brothers and sisters whenever you face trials of many kinds, because you know the testing of your faith produces perseverance." He goes on in verse 12 to say, "Blessed is the one who perseveres under trial because having stood the "test" (temptation) that person will receive the crown of life that the Lord has promised to those who love him." You must "choose" to endure the temptations of the devil, and the only way that's possible is if you have the Holy Word engraved in your heart. There is no way you can flee from temptation if you do not have the Word of God as the first resource to help withstand the attacks of the devil.

Since the foundation of the world, it was always God's prescriptive will for man not to sin. When sin entered the heart of man, God created a bridge to bring redemption through the cross. God is after your heart and soul. Nothing can ever separate us from Him. He requires that we righteously live under His Grace. As we grow in His Grace, He reveals His divine plans to us. He is able to make known to you, in the comfort of your home, your bed, your car, and the secrets of His heart! Wouldn't you want such intimacy with God?

If there were no one else on the planet, He still loves you. He wanted a relationship with you so much that He entered the world as vulnerable as can be and died on a cross for your sins. God has chosen you for great and mighty things. God is knocking on the doors of your life and wants to come and abide in your heart.

His purpose for you is far great and is very profound. The calling you have on your life is one that is irrevocable. What a privilege it is to know that God has chosen us. Despite your mess, our sins, our failures, our looks, our pedigree, God has *chosen* you. He sees you when no one else does. He knows the deepest parts of your life, and He still loves you the same. He is knocking and awaits a response. Will you let Him in? You have been *Chosen*. It is time you start living as the called, saved, sanctified, glorified chosen generation that you are.

In an age of depressing headlines and uncertainty, the Gospel (*good news*) of our Lord Jesus Christ is unchanging and unwavering. The Gospel of Jesus Christ is this; God is in love with you and me and like any lover, He wants only the best for us. God wants to share life with us and so that is why He sent His only Son Jesus to die for our salvation. He desires a lasting and impactful friendship with us. The most important ingredients of the Gospel are namely: the death, burial, and resurrection of our Lord Jesus Christ. One of the central keys is that Christ died for our sins and was raised on the third day. The true Gospel is the good news of salvation offered to mankind by grace through faith in the finished work of Christ on the cross. This good news not only guarantees eternal life but also encompasses the full plan of God. This plan includes suffering, rejoicing, restoration, grace, and the redemption from sin.

In the last decade, there has been a rise of secularism and materialism. In the United States alone, 70% of people profess Christianity as their religion. Of course, the differences between the specific denominations vary greatly, nonetheless, these are people who have their roots in Christianity. Post-World War periods, there has been a great revival of the mighty Gospel of our Lord Jesus Christ. In fact, the 1950s are known to have been some of the most powerful years for religion.

With the best of times also came some trying times. As there have been great outpourings of the Holy Spirit in our churches, there has also been the rise of many false doctrines, teachings, and theologies.

I recall a time I attended a revival during my teenage years. Eager to experience the Holy Spirit, I drove miles to hear the man of God preach. That night, he called for the whole congregation to sow 129 dollars in the ministry. By miraculous intervention, he had received a 'word' from what he said was the Holy Spirit. For almost two hours, he spoke on how the seed would bring prosperity, wealth, health and even marriages to the congregation. People shouted, claimed, and received the words. They jumped, hollowed, and many by some 'spirit' rolled on the ground. I left the service more confused than I have ever been. I was happy to give in the house of the Lord, but my expectations were not met. My spirit parched.

This was not a deliverance service nor was it a prophetic one; it was a charade. The pastor glorified himself while talking about his security guards, Rolex watches, and the many doctorate degrees he achieved. In his sermon, there was no message of the cross, self-denial, nor repentance.

---

Many have been harshly swayed from
the true Gospel.

---

Even in the wilderness, Satan tempted Jesus by offering Him all the riches and power in the world: "Again, the devil took him to a very high mountain and showed him all the kingdoms of the world and their splendor. "All this I will give you," he said, "if you will bow down and worship me" (Matthew 4:8). His scheming, deceiving ways are still as cunning as they were over 2,000 years ago. Of course, Jesus resisted and is without sin, but man has given way to these false teachings, bowing to a spirit other than that of the Holy Spirit.

Many have been harshly swayed from the *true* Gospel of our Lord Jesus Christ. Some of the largest congregations in the world are teaching a new gospel; the prosperity gospel. The prosperity theology which is often referred to as the prosperity gospel emphasizes the importance of personal empowerment through positive thoughts. This particular teaching on many levels mutes biblical teaching and reduces the Gospel of Christ to earthly promises and financial gains. The prosperity gospel, which is sometimes described as the "Word of Faith" movement, teaches that through faith, we can obtain anything we want—health, wealth, success, or whatever we please.

This force is released only through the spoken word. This movement has nothing to do with the Sovereignty of God nor does it have anything to do with the Gospel of Jesus Christ (Mark 10:45, Romans 5:8, 2 Corinthians 8:9). The "name it and claim it" gospel which I like to call it, leaves Christians empty, envious, angry and others suicidal. Perhaps you have been a participant, observer, or even a victim of this teaching. Prosperity churches have repackaged the gospel as a get-rich-quick scheme. This, in turn, leaves Christians unprepared and unaware of the true weight of purposeful Christian living.

Acts 19 records that in Ephesus, God was performing extraordinary miracles through Paul. Some of those miracles involved casting out demons from those who were possessed. He was being used by God to substantiate the Gospel of Christ and had received authority over the demons. There were also some religious charlatans who pretended to have the same ability to perform miracles.

Sceva, who was a priest at the time, had seven sons who went out trying to drive out these evil spirits as well. Envious of how God was using Paul, they decided to be the center of attention. Their plan backfired. While trying to perform their act one day, the demon responded: "Jesus I know, and Paul I know about, but who are you?" (Acts 19:15). The demon possessed man then "jumped on them and overpowered them all. He gave them such a beating that they ran out of the house naked and bleeding." The Ephesians could easily see the difference between the pretenders and the true unwavering power of Jesus Christ. Demons recognize valid authority, and most importantly, they fear God. Power of thought cannot cast out demons. The prosperity gospel cannot liberate nor does it convict of sins. This idea of the law of attraction is one that is deeply rooted in occultism. It does not only glorify the man, but it ignores the sovereignty of God.

Certainly not every teacher who preaches on the material blessings of God is a prosperity preacher. However, the Bible tells us to be very prayerful and watchful. Because of Biblical illiteracy of many Christians, they have become like prey to these teachings. Preachers of this kind pervert the truth to make it sound more appealing to the masses. The hunger for riches, prominence, and independence has left man susceptible to these sacrilegious teachings. Jesus, in His ministry, performed miracles, signs, and wonders which testified to the truth of the Gospel of our Lord.

On His resurrection, Jesus affirmed: "All authority has been given to me in heaven and on earth" (Matthew 28:18). This authority does not flow from bishops, pastors, apostles, so on and so forth. In John 16:13, we see that even the Holy Spirit does not speak for itself but only speaks what He hears. Many today are claiming "thus says the Lord" when in reality, the carnality of their minds will not allow their spirits to connect to the Spirit of God.

Our world today makes it easy to feel entitled to the luxury car, the new phone, the exotic vacation, and much more. This makes it easy for those who take part in the prosperity teachings to feel entitled before God. In turn, many have stopped approaching God with a humble and contrite heart, but rather with a pompous attitude, expecting blessings. God promises blessings to those who serve him faithfully and follow his statutes. In Malachi 3:10-11, God says "bring the whole tithe into the storehouse, that there may be food in my house. Test me in this," says the Lord Almighty, "and see if I will not throw open the floodgates of heaven and pour out so much blessing that there will not be room enough to store it!" This is God speaking His promises unto us.

Wealth and health are not inherently sinful. In fact, wealth creation and proper management of money can cause one to flourish. Material blessings were part of the Mosaic and Judaic Covenants for Israel. The prosperity gospel being preached today, however, showcases men and not God. It teaches that wealth and holiness are innately connected and it glorifies earthly treasures above salvation. The imbalanced focus on earthly treasure is in direct contrast to the many passages that warn us not to desire riches. Prosperity teachings focus on these three key points: faith, wealth, and health. The faith they proclaim many times does not focus on the proclaimed Word of God but rather encourages positive thoughts with the results being material blessings. This is not the *true* Gospel of our Lord and Savior.

In the Book of 1 Timothy 6:9, we see how detrimental this can be because

> "Godliness with contentment is great gain. For we brought nothing into the world, and we can take nothing out of it. But if we have food and clothing, we will be content with that. Those who want to get rich fall into temptation and a trap and into many foolish and harmful desires that plunge people into ruin and destruction. For the love of money is a root of all kinds of evil. Some people, eager for money, have wandered from the faith and pierced themselves with many griefs."

Many have the envy to get rich quick. They are diluted with a false reality and are blindly led away from the truth. Riches are not always a sign of God's blessings. Flocks of people are traveling and even flying hundreds of miles a year to attend mega 'supernatural' revivals and mega-churches that teach them how to *feel good* as a Christian. As predicted in 2 Timothy 4:4, they have turned away their ears from the truth, and have turned towards the *feel-good* message.

God has called every one of us to deny ourselves and pick up the Cross and follow Him. Whether rich or poor, sick or healthy, He wants *you!* God's perfect will for us may not seem perfect to us and will not always feel good. He did not promise that He would give us mansions and millions on this earth. Many say, well, Christ came poor that we may be rich!

Yes, the Word of God does say this. However, Christ also commanded us to be strong and not be surprised at the fiery ordeal that has come on us to test us (1 Peter 4:12). Jesus Christ said in John 14:3; He has gone to prepare a place for you and me. He will come back to take us with Him. Prosperity teachers focus mainly on our survival on this earth through health and riches. As Paul points out, there is a heavy cost for following Jesus Christ. The journey is not all glitz and glam.

> "Five times I received from the Jews the forty lashes minus one. Three times I was beaten with rods, once I was pelted with stones, three times I was shipwrecked, I spent a night and a day in the open sea, I have been constantly on the move. I have been in danger from rivers, in danger from bandits, in danger from my fellow Jews, in danger from Gentiles; in danger in the city, in danger in the country, in danger at sea; and in danger from false believers. I have labored and toiled and have often gone without sleep; I have known hunger and thirst and have often gone without food; I have been cold and naked. Besides everything else, I face daily the pressure of my concern for all the churches." (2 Cor 11:24-28)

The true Gospel of Christ requires sacrifice. It is a glorious yet painful and satisfying journey. As we learn to deny the flesh and live in the Spirit, the Holy Spirit works as our counselor to shape us that we may be perfected in God's will. Tithing and giving are biblical principles for Christian living. However, we should tithe and give with a cheerful spirit, not one that has been coerced and manipulated. In all we do, we should seek the spiritual blessing of salvation before the material blessing of wealth.

God is in the pursuit of your heart and desires that you will be saved through His Son Jesus. He will not leave you ignorant of His plans for you. The Bible has been written as a blueprint to eternal life. You have a choice to make. As God has *chosen* you to be part of His marvelous story line, accept Him to be a part of yours. He is standing at the door and is knocking. He will not force Himself in. Accepting His plans His will and His way is the best decision you can ever make. Once you allow God to be a part of your story, your life will never be the same. Your purpose will be clear and your focus will be sharpened. Chose God as He Himself has *chosen* you.

*It is God's will for every one of His children to know Christ Jesus.*

# <u>SALVATION PRAYER</u>

Dear God in heaven, I come to you in the name of Jesus. I acknowledge to You that I am a sinner, and I am sorry for my sins. I know the life that I have lived has not been up to your standards. I need your forgiveness. I acknowledge the completed work of Your Son, Jesus Christ, in giving His life for me on the cross at Calvary, and I long to receive the forgiveness you have made freely available to me through this sacrifice. Come into my life now, Lord. Take up residence in my heart and be my king, my Lord, and my Savior. From this day forward, I will no longer be controlled by sin, or the desire to please myself, but I will follow You all the days of my life. Those days are in Your hands. I ask this in Jesus' precious and holy name. Amen.

# VERSES FOR MEDITATION

For by grace you have been saved through faith. And this is not your own doing; it is the gift of God.

*-Ephesians 2:8*

Let us then with confidence draw near to the throne of grace, that we may receive mercy and find grace to help in time of need.

*-Hebrews 4:16*

But if it is by grace, it is no longer on the basis of works; otherwise grace would no longer be grace.

*-Romans 11:6*

Here I am! I stand at the door and knock. If anyone hears my voice and opens the door, I will come in and eat with him, and he with me.

*-Revelation 3:20*

Jesus answered, "I am the way and the truth and the life. No one comes to the father except through me."

*-John 14:6*

Therefore, if anyone is in Christ he is a new creation; the old has gone, the new has come!

*-2 Corinthians 5:17*

And we know that in all things God works for the good of those who love him, who have been called according to his purpose.

*-Romans 8:28*

For I am convinced that neither death nor life, neither angels nor demons, neither the present nor the future, nor any powers, neither height nor depth, nor anything else in all creation, will be able to separate us from the love of God that is in Christ Jesus our Lord.

*-Romans 8:38-39*

"For I know the plans I have for you," declares the Lord, "plans to prosper you and not to harm you, plans to give you hope and a future."

*-Jeremiah 29:11*

But he said to me, "My grace is sufficient for you, for my power is made perfect in weakness." Therefore I will boast all the more gladly about my weaknesses, so that Christ's power may rest on me.

*-2 Corinthians 12:9*

Delight yourself in the Lord and he will give you the desires of your heart. Commit your way to the Lord, trust in him and he will do this.

*-Psalm 37:4,5*

I can do all things through Christ who strengthens me.

*-Philippians 4:13*

But the fruit of the Spirit is love, joy, peace, patience, kindness, goodness, faithfulness, gentleness and self-control. Against such things there is no law.

*- Galatians 5:22-23*

Do not be anxious about anything, but in everything, by prayer and petition, with thanksgiving, present your requests to God. And the peace of God, which transcends all understanding, will guard your hearts and your minds in Christ Jesus.

*-Philippians 4:6-7*

All Scripture is God-breathed and is useful for teaching, rebuking, correcting, and training in righteousness.

*-2 Timothy 3:16*

If we confess our sins, he is faithful and just and will forgive us our sins and purify us from all unrighteousness.

*-1 John 1:9*

No temptation has seized you except what is common to man. And God is faithful; he will not let you be tempted beyond what you can bear. But when you are tempted, he will also provide a way out, so that you can stand up under it.

*-1 Corinthians 10:13*

This Book of the Law shall not depart from your mouth, but you shall meditate in it day and night, that you may observe to do according to all that is written in it. For then you will make your way prosperous, and then you will have good success.

*-Joshua 1:8*

Whenever I am afraid, I will trust in You

*-Psalm 56:3*

You will keep him in perfect peace, Whose mind is stayed on You, Because he trusts in You.

*-Isaiah 26:3*

And we know that all things work together for good to those who love God, to those who are the called according to His purpose.

*-Romans 8:28*

But those who wait on the LORD Shall renew their strength; They shall mount up with wings like eagles, They shall run and not be weary, They shall walk and not faint.

*-Isaiah 40:31*

Through the LORD'S mercies we are not consumed, Because His compassions fail not. They are new every morning; Great is Your faithfulness.

*-Lamentations 3:22-23*

But seek first the kingdom of God and His righteousness, and all these things shall be added to you. "Therefore do not worry about tomorrow, for tomorrow will worry about its own things. Sufficient for the day is its own trouble.

*- Matthew 6:33-34*

Then Jesus said to His disciples, "If anyone desires to come after Me, let him deny himself, and take up his cross, and follow Me. "For whoever desires to save his life will lose it, but whoever loses his life for My sake will find it. "For what profit is it to a man if he gains the whole world, and loses his own soul? Or what will a man give in exchange for his soul?

*-Matthew 16:24-26*

If you abide in Me, and My words abide in you, you will ask what you desire, and it shall be done for you.

*-John 15:7*

There is therefore now no condemnation to those who are in Christ Jesus, who do not walk according to the flesh, but according to the Spirit.

*-Romans 8:1*

If you confess with your mouth the Lord Jesus and believe in your heart that God has raised Him from the dead, you will be saved. For with the heart one believes unto righteousness, and with the mouth confession is made unto salvation.

*-Romans 10:9-10*

For God so loved the world that he gave his one and only Son, that whoever believes in him shall not perish but have eternal life

*-John 3:16*

Trust in the LORD with all your heart and lean not on your own understanding.

*-Proverbs 3:5*

I have been crucified with Christ and I no longer live, but Christ lives in me. The life I live in the body, I live by faith in the Son of God, who loved me and gave himself for me.

*-Galatians 2:20*

Have I not commanded you? Be strong and courageous. Do not be terrified; do not be discouraged, for the LORD your God will be with you wherever you go.

*-Joshua 1:9*

But he was pierced for our transgressions, he was crushed for our iniquities; the punishment that brought us peace was upon him, and by his wounds we are healed.

*-Isaiah 53:5*

So do not fear, for I am with you; do not be dismayed, for I am your God. I will strengthen you and help you; I will uphold you with my righteous right hand.

*-Isaiah 6:10*

So now I am giving you a new commandment: Love each other.  Just as I have loved you, you should love each other.  Your love for one another will prove to the world that you are my disciples.

*- John 13:34-35*

There is no fear in love. But perfect love drives out fear, because fear has to do with punishment.  The one who fears is not made perfect in love.  We love because He first loved us.

*-John 4:18-19*

Love must be sincere. Hate what is evil; cling to what is good. Be devoted to one another in brotherly love. Honor one another above yourselves.

*-Romans 12:9-10*

And he called to him his twelve disciples and gave them authority over unclean spirits, to cast them out, and to heal every disease and every affliction.

*-Matthew 10:1*

My son, be attentive to my words; incline your ear to my sayings. Let them not escape from your sight; keep them within your heart. For they are life to those who find them, and healing to all their flesh.

*-Proverbs 4:20-22*

And the Lord will take away from you all sickness, and none of the evil diseases of Egypt, which you knew, will he inflict on you, but he will lay them on all who hate you.

*-Deuteronomy 7:15*

No weapon that is fashioned against you shall succeed, and you shall confute every tongue that rises against you in judgment. This is the heritage of the servants of the Lord and their vindication from me, declares the Lord."

*-Isaiah 54:17*

I have seen his ways, but I will heal him; I will lead him and restore comfort to him and his mourners, creating the fruit of the lips. Peace, peace, to the far and to the near," says the Lord, "and I will heal him.

*-Isaiah 57:18-19*

For to this you have been called, because Christ also suffered for you, leaving you an example, so that you might follow in his steps. He committed no sin, neither was deceit found in his mouth. When he was reviled, he did not revile in return; when he suffered, he did not threaten, but continued entrusting himself to him who judges justly. He himself bore our sins in his body on the tree, that we might die to sin and live to righteousness. By his wounds you have been healed.

*-1 Peter 2:21-24*

If my people who are called by my name humble themselves, and pray and seek my face and turn from their wicked ways, then I will hear from heaven and will forgive their sin and heal their land.

*-2 Chronicles 7:14*

You make known to me the path of life; in your presence there is fullness of joy; at your right hand are pleasures forevermore.

*-Psalm 16:11*

Though you have not seen him, you love him. Though you do not now see him, you believe in him and rejoice with joy that is inexpressible and filled with glory, obtaining the outcome of your faith, the salvation of your souls.

*-1 Peter 1:8-9*

Now to him who is able to keep you from stumbling and to present you blameless before the presence of his glory with great joy,

*-Jude 1:24*

And the ransomed of the Lord shall return and come to Zion with singing; everlasting joy shall be upon their heads; they shall obtain gladness and joy, and sorrow and sighing shall flee away.

*-Isaiah 35:10*

*END*

www.rebeccamerzius.com

*Instagram: rebeccamerzius*

*Facebook: rebeccamerzius*

Rebecca is excited to share the Gospel with your group or congregation. For speaking or preaching inquiries, please email rebecca.merzius@gmail.com and the team will respond accordingly.